"Memory is often discussed by scien[t] nating subject into dry prose. Howev[e] to life, continually returning to the q [...] *tion?* He explores different forms of m [...] the power of sensing, attending, and rehearsing, and identifies various chokepoints, such as the pitfalls of multitasking. He also reveals how students often fail to choose the most effective study methods. The most exciting part comes with his discussion on maximizing learning, where he details numerous effective techniques, providing practical advice and examples, all rooted in his teaching experiences. A powerful, beautifully written overview of what really matters to develop student learning."

John Hattie, Emeritus Laureate Professor, and author of the *Visible Learning* series

"Human cognition is complex. Applying our knowledge of human cognition to instructional procedures is more complex. Explaining it in an intelligible fashion is herculean. Blake Harvard has brilliantly accomplished this explanatory task. I recommend this book to all engaged in the teaching profession."

John Sweller, Emeritus Professor of Educational Psychology, and Father of Cognitive Load Theory

"Brimming with classroom-ready techniques grounded in cognitive research, every educator will find multiple ideas in this marvelous little volume that will improve their practice and deepen their insights into their students."

Daniel T. Willingham, Professor of Psychology, and author of *Why Don't Students Like School?*

"I am pretty picky when it comes to teacher books purporting to represent cognitive science. In this book, Blake Harvard leaps above the pack of books on this topic and comes out as among the best books I've encountered. I've long desired a book-length treatment of Dr. Stephen Chew's "pitfalls and chokepoints" diagram, and that's just what Blake has provided here. As a teacher and a thinker, I can't recommend the book, or Blake's blog, enough."

Dave Stuart Jr., author of *The Will to Learn: How to Cultivate Student Motivation without Losing Our Own*

"Over the last few years, a revolution has been taking place in classrooms, where the science behind learning, motivation, focus and memory has crept into the classroom, displacing the mysticism and superstition that previously dominated. But this hasn't happened by accident – it takes the hard work of thoughtful, practical people who understand the need to translate theory into practice, and research into reality. One of the best voices who practise this bilingualism is Blake Harvard, one of a new wave of authors who have made evidence-informed education something that hard-working teachers and leaders can understand, and crucially, implement. This book is a superb addition to the modern canon of research-informed education, and I wish every teacher was familiar with its pages."

Tom Bennett, founder of researchED

DO I HAVE YOUR ATTENTION?

Do I Have Your Attention? explores memory processing, how students learn, and offers practical guidance to help teachers tailor their instruction to be the most efficient and effective for learning.

Drawing on evidence from cognitive science, Part I offers an easy-to-understand explanation of the process of memory and highlights certain barriers that hinder students' ability to learn. Part II introduces over a century of research into two widely applicable learning strategies and, drawing on the author's extensive teaching experience, demonstrates a plethora of classroom applications that maximize learning while working within the known constraints of human memory.

Part of The InnerDrive Teacher CPD Academy series that offers a deep dive into the key areas that matter to teachers, this is essential reading for all teachers and school leaders who want evidence-based strategies which focus on impact in the classroom in sustainable and meaningful ways.

Blake Harvard is a teacher at James Clemens High School in Madison, Alabama, USA.

The Teacher CPD Academy
Series editors: Bradley Busch and Edward Watson

The Homework Conundrum
How to Stop the Dog From Eating Homework
Jovita M. Castelino

Do I Have Your Attention?
Understanding Memory Constraints and Maximizing Learning
Blake Harvard

DO I HAVE YOUR ATTENTION?

Understanding Memory Constraints and Maximizing Learning

Blake Harvard

 Routledge
Taylor & Francis Group

LONDON AND NEW YORK

Designed cover image: © InnerDrive

First published 2025
by Routledge
4 Park Square, Milton Park, Abingdon, Oxon OX14 4RN

and by Routledge
605 Third Avenue, New York, NY 10158

Routledge is an imprint of the Taylor & Francis Group, an informa business

British Library Cataloguing-in-Publication Data
A catalogue record for this book is available from the British Library

ISBN: 978-1-032-75028-6 (hbk)
ISBN: 978-1-032-75027-9 (pbk)
ISBN: 978-1-003-47205-6 (ebk)

DOI: 10.4324/9781003472056

Typeset in Interstate
by KnowledgeWorks Global Ltd.

Printed and bound in Great Britain by Bell and Bain Ltd, Glasgow

To Mom and Dad.

To Jenny.

To Eli, Hattie, Janie,

and Gus. Woof.

CONTENTS

FOREWORD

It is a great privilege to write the foreword to *Do I Have Your Attention?* Having been a huge fan of Blake's blogs and live presentations for a number of years, we consider ourselves truly lucky that he agreed to write his debut book as part of our "Teacher CPD Academy" series.

In a world filled with information and misinformation, now more than ever we need people who can expertly translate complex research into a format that is both accessible and applicable. And for us, when it comes to cognitive science, no-one does it better than Blake Harvard.

Do I Have Your Attention? explores one of the perennial problems in education; how do the constraints of human cognitive architecture impact on student learning, and crucially, what can we do to help students manage these? To answer this, this book will take you on a thrilling tour on seminal research on attention, working memory, multi-tasking, cognitive load, retrieval, and spacing.

Understanding how learning happens is fundamental to great teaching. With great clarity, Blake describes the research around the former before providing practical strategies on the latter. Combining his knowledge of a wealth of studies with years of practical experience in the classroom, he is uniquely positioned to write this book. And the education landscape is all the more better for it.

As with all books in this series, we have an accompanying module on this topic on our online platform www.teachercpdacademy.com. Along with Blake's on Attention and Memory, you can find a range of topics on teaching and learning, which include modules, keynotes, interviews with researchers, and lesson materials.

We hope that this book, and the whole series, illuminates key research, inspires reflection, and sparks discussions. If it does that, then ultimately it will improve and enrich the lives of your students.

Bradley Busch and Edward Watson,
Directors of InnerDrive.

PREFACE

First, and foremost, I am a classroom teacher. More than I am an author or researcher or conference presenter, I am a teacher. When asked "what do you teach?", I respond with "psychology," which is true, but I also teach my students about many other matters that are psychology-adjacent. The topics may not be typed into the prescribed curriculum, but definitely apply to student success in both life and learning. This mostly centers around cognition, memory, and learning. I am incredibly passionate about how our brain works and how we both remember and forget information. You can often find me reading and writing about different learning strategies that, evidence demonstrates, may be advantageous for learning in the classroom.

As a teacher, I want to know how to instruct so that students have the best opportunities for experiencing, understanding, organizing, and remembering material. There are seemingly countless questions to be asked when considering this. How can I best present material and have students interact, use, manipulate, and apply the information? How should I structure the classroom? Where should students sit? How many posters should I have on the wall? Should I do most of the talking? Should students teach each other? How many questions should I ask? Are worksheets a good idea? How many projects should students complete during the semester?

If you are a teacher, you've probably had many of these questions (and a lot more) swirling through your head at one time or another. On the one hand, teaching and learning can appear to be quite simple; get the information to the students and have them use the information. On the other hand, it can be incredibly complicated as we see with the previous questions. Add to this the fact that every classroom and learner is different. The number of changing variables in any classroom on a given day is staggering. Just considering learners' abilities, attitudes, consciousness, and motivation can completely impact the effectiveness of instruction. Also, what may work with third-grade students in rural Iowa may have little or no effects on learning in an inner-city high school in London.

And there is no silver bullet in education...including this book. There, I said it. Any presenter, author, and/or consultant who tries to tell you they have THE way to educate is either vastly misinformed or trying to take advantage of you. Trust me, if researchers had discovered an all-encompassing strategy or system that worked for learners of all ages and abilities, it would've been packaged nicely and sold to you and your school district with a nice price tag attached to it. Nothing works all of the time for all students. This book isn't trying to be everything for every student, because it simply cannot be.

This book is meant to provide, for many teachers, a somewhat different focus on instruction and learning. Cognitive psychology offers many insights into how people learn and what makes for more effective and efficient learning. Talking with many teachers around the globe, it is obvious that much of the information in this book is absent from teacher training programs. I believe this to be a massive oversight in education. It borders on malpractice that a majority of educators (especially those in the United States) have never been instructed, themselves, on different aspects of memory and learning. Perhaps the main job of a teacher is to teach students information; that students exit a classroom knowing and understanding more than when they walked in. How can this best be accomplished if we don't know what conditions best capitalize on remembering? This, in a nutshell, embodies the major goal of this book; to fill this gap in teacher education...from a teacher who is living this out every day in the classroom.

While I am very thankful for the education I received while in college, I graduated without any classes or training on memory. So, for the first decade of my teaching career, I now feel as though I didn't really provide the most effective and efficient classroom. It wasn't until 2016, when I ran across The Learning Scientists, on Twitter. I don't remember the exact tweet or article I read that sparked my interest, but I do remember that feeling of "oh, yeah, this seems logical and applicable in my classroom." The general aim and scope of the entire website just made sense. Instead of just shooting in the dark with my instruction, here was information and research showing evidence of effectiveness with learning strategies. I remember being instantly drawn to the material and feeling as though I'd found a diamond in the rough. It wasn't until later that I discovered the researchers who ran the site were cognitive psychologists from around the world. Before I knew it, I was tweeting back and forth with the account and had accepted an offer to write a guest blog for the site, something I'd never done before. After doing a bit of research, myself, and nervously writing the article, I knew I was hooked. I loved discovering a topic, finding research, and considering how the results from this study may apply to the learners in my classroom. I very quickly started my own website, and I've been reading research articles and writing about the application of cognitive psychology in the classroom ever since.

As I said earlier, though, there is no silver bullet in education. Cognitive psychology is not the be-all-end-all of education. There are other aspects of learning that should be taken into account when developing and implementing instruction. What I appreciate about findings from cognitive psychology is its adaptability to differing subject material, ability levels, and age ranges. As a result, the research and strategies discussed in the book don't apply to only a psychology class, math class, or science class. They are useful for any curriculum and age group. Cognitive psychology isn't about a particular subject, but, more generally, how we think and learn and remember.

Before concluding, I believe it necessary in a text about education to define what is meant by learning. For this, I turn to Drs. Kirschner, Sweller, and Clark: *learning is a change in long-term memory*.[1] If there has been no changes and additions to a student's long-term memory, with respect to subject material, nothing has been learned. Students should leave class knowing more than when they entered. This requires a change in long-term memory. If this seems a bit foreign to you, don't worry, it will be further discussed in Part I.

My sincere hope is that the information in this book provides an "ah-ha" moment for you like The Learning Scientists did for me and simplifies how you think about instruction. I hope it provides a new lens to view the classroom environment and learning in the classroom. I know over the past years that incorporating lessons from cognitive psychology has made my instruction more organized and enriched learning in my classroom. I truly hope it does the same for yours; from one classroom teacher to another.

Note

1 Kirschner, P. A., Sweller, J., & Clark, R. E. (2006). Why minimal guidance during instruction does not work: An analysis of the failure of constructivist, discovery, problem-based, experiential, and inquiry-based teaching. *Educational Psychologist, 41,* 75–86.

PART I
Understanding Memory Constraints

The quote "Without knowledge of human cognitive processes, instructional design is blind."[1] hit me like a ton of bricks. It is the first sentence in an incredibly technical and important text on learning and cognition. It was very clearly one of those instances where you read something that is both so simple and so profound that you can almost quite literally feel the lightbulb click on in your head. And in the next instance, I think I felt a bit ashamed in myself as a teacher. How did I not see this earlier? Of course, if I'm creating lessons which involve learners interacting with and using material both visually and auditorily, I must consider human cognitive processes; I must consider how memory works and how we learn. Without doing so, I'm sort of throwing darts in the dark; just hoping to hit the target of learning and never really knowing which hit and which miss.

Much of what we do, with respect to designing and implementing instruction, involves attempting to impart information to students in hopes they can first remember and then use that knowledge in some form or fashion; maybe it's on a quiz, during a discussion, or to create or invent a new product. *How can we provide the most efficient and effective lessons if we don't understand what happens from the time students hear and/or see the information to the time it is needed for use?* Part I provides a basic understanding of different processes of memory and roadblocks that may impede learning. Simply put, this information is indispensable for the teacher (and student). So, let's take the blindfold

DOI: 10.4324/9781003472056-1

off while designing instruction and work within what we know about memory processing to maximize the learning in our classrooms.

Note

1 Sweller, J., Ayres, P., & Kalyuga, S. (2011). *Cognitive load theory*. Springer.

1 Memory Processing

The graphic on the next page represents memory processing. And it is just that...a process. There are a few different types of memory along the path from sensory memory to long-term memory, and there are both limitations and roadblocks we may experience along the way to stymie learning. At first glance, the image can be overwhelming, especially if you've never considered memory processing. There are a lot of arrows and words that may seem a little foreign. But don't fret, Part I is completely dedicated to explaining this process and, trust me, it is worth your time. I guarantee, when you're finished, you'll wonder why this is (potentially) the first time you're seeing this information and wonder how much more efficient and effective you can educate your students (and yourself) by understanding how memory works. Think about this process working from top to bottom. The goal in the classroom is to begin by sensing the necessary information (at the top) and work through the process until the information is stored and accessible in long-term memory (at the bottom).

Sensory Memory

Incoming information (stimuli that are sensed) is first registered in *sensory memory*. In the classroom, this usually equates to either auditory or visual sensation since content is usually communicated either verbally or visually. Humans sense much more than we can attend to and perceive. Most stimuli in sensory memory are forgotten. Although our eyes and ears

DOI: 10.4324/9781003472056-2

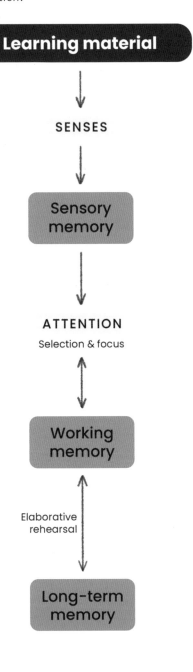

are constantly sensing millions of bits of information, we can consciously only attend to a few. For instance, you are (hopefully) consciously attending to the words you are reading right now. But there are light waves in your periphery that are still entering your eye and being processed by the rods and cones in your retina. However, you are not paying that periphery visual sensation any attention, and you have no chance to remember that sensory information. Visually, you are only consciously aware of the words on this paper, and this information is the only explicit material you might remember. All other visual sensation will almost immediately be forgotten.

Similarly, you are also sensing a multitude of differing sounds at this very moment. Pause for a second and listen for the many different sources of auditory sensations. Maybe it's the sound of the air conditioner in the room, perhaps the sound of a ticking clock, people talking nearby, cars just outside, et cetera. Depending on where you are, there could be numerous sources of sound. And those soundwaves are surely entering your ear and eventually being processed in the temporal lobes of your brain. But, just like visual stimuli, if you are not attending to those sounds, they are very quickly fading from your memory and are gone. So, if you choose to focus on the sound of the air conditioner, you cannot also attend to the sound of the clock ticking. And we cannot really "rewind the tape" for any worthwhile length of time with respect to sensory memory. Once it's gone, it's gone. So, while sensation of material in the classroom is a necessary first step, by itself, it is not enough to remember anything.

Attention

This brings us to a major aspect of memory and the main focus of this book, *attention*. Among the myriad of sensations we experience at any given time, attention is the necessary next step in memory processing. Attention is like currency. It is a limited resource, and we choose how to spend it, just like we spend our time, energy, and money. If we choose, either consciously or unconsciously, to attend to one form of stimuli in our environment, we are also making the decision to ignore other stimuli. So, creating learning environments that are conducive to focusing attention on particular material or resources is superior to those where there is no clear understanding of what is important or environments where multiple distractors are present.

Working Memory

So, the material has been sensed, and it is being attended to by students. The next necessary step in the process of remembering is *working memory*. Quite simply, whatever you are consciously thinking about right now is what is in your working memory. I tell my students it's the information your brain is working with at this moment. If I asked you to think about what you ate for dinner last night, the memory of that meal is now in your working memory. But, since last night's plate of food is currently occupying your working memory, no other memories can be processed or consciously attended to. It's a bit like a bottleneck for memory. Information from sensory memory that is attended to must enter working memory but only so much can possibly be processed at any given time to eventually move to long-term memory...more on that later.

While this working memory store is more durable than sensory memory, it is still quite fleeting and information decays quite rapidly. It is limited both in the amount of information that can be stored at any time and in the length of time it can be stored without either decaying (being forgotten) or continuing on in the process to long-term memory.

Limitations of Working Memory

The limited capacity of working memory is often cited as either being between five and nine bits of information[1] or, more recently, defined as being around four "chunks" of information.[2] A bit of information might be an individual number or term to be remembered. A chunk, in this instance, may be represented as short sentences or idioms; more than a single letter, but not entire paragraphs of information. It may also be something like an idea or a concept. This number of four chunks can either decrease or increase depending on the complexity and familiarity of the information. The more familiar a student may be with a concept in class, the more chunks of new material they may be able to hold in working memory at one time. And, conversely, the absence of adequate background knowledge of a particular concept or process being learned can more quickly fill the limited amount of space in working memory.

There are easy ways to demonstrate this in the classroom with students. I usually begin by verbally giving my students a list of four random digits between one and nine. After telling the students, I have them write the numbers down in order. Generally speaking, they do really well with the list of four. Around 90% will list all in order. Next, I'll provide five different digits to remember and then write down. Again, this is relatively easy. This continues for six, seven, eight, nine, and ten numbers. It is around seven digits that students begin to struggle. And, increasingly so with eight, nine, and ten, to the point that maybe only one student will successfully write down nine and ten digits correctly. This illustrates the idea that working memory capacity is limited to really only around five to nine digits.

Then, I provide one more opportunity for students to hear a list of ten digits and ask them to write the numbers down in order. This time is a little different, though. It is a phone number. And, how the numbers are chunked together assists the students with remembering all ten digits. And where only maybe one of thirty students remembered all ten on the first attempt, around 50% will remember all ten digits when they are chunked together and the first three digits (the area code) are familiar.

Applying this to the limitations of working memory's capacity, when the students are familiar with the first three numbers of the ten number sequence and can mentally assign them the category of "area code," they have turned those three unrelated bits of information into one chunk of information and have lowered the load this information occupies in working memory, making room for more information to be processed. This demonstration also highlights the importance of background knowledge in the learning of new, related material. It is much easier to add to information you already know because the load of the new material will occupy less space in working memory and cognitively be chunked to the information that is already related in long-term memory. With completely new content, working memory is much more easily overloaded because there's really no background knowledge or related information to chunk the new material to.

The other limitation of working memory capacity refers to the amount of time that information will remain in memory. Depending on the sensation, stimuli persist in working memory for around 15–30 seconds.[3] After that time, it is either forgotten or rehearsed and begins the move to being processed in long-term memory. This is also quite easy to demonstrate with students. Simply go back and ask them to recall the five-digit number from the activity above after finishing with the last ten-digit number. It is possible that one or two may recall the digits, but a vast majority will fail this simple test. Obviously, at some point, the numbers were sensed, attended to, and in their working memory if the students were able to initially write it down. But, over time (more than 30 seconds) and without rehearsal of the item, the numbers are forgotten.

So, like other aspects of memory processing thus far, information being held in our conscious, working memory is a necessary step, but it is insufficient for long-term remembering of information. And, as I'm sure you understand, one of the main goals of education is for our students to learn, understand, and use the information we teach for much longer than 30 seconds.

Long-Term Memory

That brings us to *long-term memory*. To the best of our knowledge, the capacity of long-term memory is limitless. As I tell my students, no one has filled up their brain so much that if they learn one more fact, other information is going to start falling out their ears. To further demonstrate this point, I introduce my students to individuals with highly superior autobiographical memory (HSAM). These people have the ability to recall, with incredible accuracy, seemingly innocuous events from weeks, months, and years past. One video I show in class asks a person to recall the days it rained in New York City from months and years ago...and they did so correctly.[4] If these people haven't filled up their brain with information, the rest of us are in no danger of doing so. Long-term memory is the only store house not limited by capacity, as an innumerable amount of information may be stored here, and it may be remembered for many decades.

While it would be fantastic if the memories of classroom material automatically (without conscious effort) processed into long-term memory and just stayed there until they needed to be recalled, that is usually not the case. The vast majority of information we present to students to learn and remember is explicit in nature. These memories are also sometimes called declarative memories because we can declare we know them. Explicit memories require effortful processing and are not automatically processed and remembered in long-term memory.

There are many different methods to elicit effortful processing of information in the classroom, all of them boiling down to requiring students to use the information in some form or fashion. Sometimes that may just be filling in a blank with a correct term. It may also manifest itself as using specific knowledge in a debate to prove a point or demonstrating the understanding of a topic to hypothesize future events. Basically, due to the nature of the material being taught in the classroom, cognitive effort is necessary for the remembering of material.

Looking back at the memory processing model a few pages back, you see the arrow between working memory and long-term memory moves back and forth. This illustrates how a memory, once accessed from long-term memory, is now in use with a person's working memory. Again, it is what they are working with at that moment. Asking students to recall what they ate for breakfast that morning demonstrates this mental experience. The memory of their bowl of cereal was stored in long-term memory but is now consciously in their working memory. By allowing a memory, over time, to repeatedly be recalled from long-term memory and moved into working memory and then back to long-term memory may actually physically strengthen those connections in the brain and make access to that memory more durable, efficient, and effective. This is called long-term potentiation.[5]

In the classroom, the more we require students to recall content and correctly apply it in class or during homework opportunities, the stronger those memories become and the easier they will be retrieved the next instance they need that material. This has major implications for designing instruction and learning activities in the classroom that will be discussed in Part II.

A Spider Web of Knowledge

At this point, I think it is helpful to illustrate how memories are organized in the brain. For one reason or another, most associate the saving of memories in the brain like that of files on a computer; each in their own precise and discrete location. But this is simply not the case. I like to think of it more like a spider web. A web that has more connections and is more complex will be much stronger than a web with fewer and will do a better job at catching bugs. The web that has very few attachments is more fragile and simply doesn't have the same ability to trap any bugs that may fly into it.

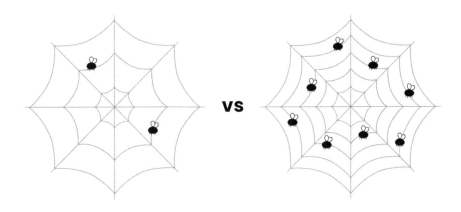

Memories are quite similar. Rather than being stored independently, memories of similarly related material are connected. These connections equate to context surrounding the memory. If I asked you to again recall the breakfast you ate this morning, you don't simply remember the bowl of cereal. You can also remember the context as well; the room you were in, the table you might have been seated at, what was on the television, who was sitting with you, et cetera. All of those other details surrounding the seemingly singular memory you were intending to recall make that spider web more complex and those memories stronger and easier to access.

This also helps to explain the importance of background knowledge in the learning of new information. If I already have a well-established spider web of knowledge about a particular topic, it is easier to "catch" new information. I can more easily incorporate that content and build upon what I already know. However, if I know little to nothing about the topic (thus having a very basic and fragile spider web), it is much harder to "catch" and remember the new information and understand its meaning. And, when we access memories, not only do we strengthen the context and connections we have already established, we also add new context, which makes the spider web even more complex.

Episodic Context Account

This adding of new contexts aiding in the ability to retrieve information is described by Dr. Jeffrey Karpicke as the episodic context account.[6] Basically, the more a person attempts to recall information in differing contexts, the more potential different "context features" are added to that web of information about that particular subject. In my metaphor, this equates to added links in the spider web. And, as previously stated, the more context (and web) we have surrounding a particular topic, the easier it may be to retrieve that information. This added context also provides more potential retrieval cues for the material. And, as will be explained in greater detail later, the more retrieval cues we have for a particular bit of information, the easier it may be to get that material out of long-term memory and in to working memory for usage by the student.

Chapter 1 provided a somewhat brief overview for how memory processing works. While it is extremely important for teachers to understand this process and consider how this could impact instruction, it is also advantageous for our students to also be introduced to and comprehend how they learn. Chapter 2 discusses how I frame this discussion for my students.

Notes

1 Miller, G. A. (1956). The magical number seven, plus or minus two: Some limits on our capacity for processing information. *Psychological Review, 63*(2), 81.

2 Cowan, N. (2010). The magical mystery four: How is working memory capacity limited, and why? *Current Directions in Psychological Science, 19*(1), 51–57.

3 Weinstein, Y. (2017, June 17). *How long is short-term memory? Shorter than you might think*. The Learning Scientists. https://www.learningscientists.org/blog/2017/4/13-1

4 60 Minutes Australia. (2019, September 21). *People who remember every second of their life* [Video]. YouTube. https://www.youtube.com/watch?v=hpTCZ-hO6iI

5 Shors, T. J., & Matzel, L. D. (1997). Long-term potentiation: What's learning got to do with it? *Behavioral and Brain Sciences, 20*(4), 597–614.

6 Karpicke, J. D., Lehman, M., & Aue, W. R. (2014). Retrieval-based learning: An episodic context account. *Psychology of learning and motivation* (Vol. 61, pp. 237–284). Academic Press.

2 The SAR Method

While it is certainly a worthwhile endeavor to have a basic understanding of memory processing and how it impacts learning whether you are a teacher or student, I also understand that time is an incredibly limited resource in the classroom. I doubt many teachers have extra lessons to devote to introducing all of the information in Chapter 1 to their students. I am lucky that it is included in my curriculum as a psychology teacher. With that in mind, I created a method for understanding major aspects of memory. Not only does it simplify the process, but it is quite applicable for early years through college aged learners.

It's simple, easy to remember, and I believe it isn't too technical. Also, I think it provides an easy avenue for students to consider what actions they control when thinking about their learning environment and studying. It's just three words, and I believe the simplicity makes it more likely students (and teachers) would be more likely to apply it to their learning and teaching. Some of this is a rehashing of what has been written previously, but I think it is valuable to see how it is described to students for their understanding.

DOI: 10.4324/9781003472056-3

Sense

Without a doubt, the first step is sensation. One must sense the information to have any chance of continuing through the memory process. If you do not sense the material (in the classroom, this usually means hearing it and/or seeing it), there is no chance of perceiving the material; unless you have extrasensory perception...and you don't.

But, of course, just sensing the information isn't enough. We are constantly sensing a plethora of stimuli every second of our life, and there is no chance we remember all of it. For instance, right now, wherever you are reading this, there are numerous sources of auditory stimuli. Just stop reading for a second and consider all of the different sounds you're hearing. And, while all of those sound waves are making their way through the air, into your ear, and eventually to your brain, that is not enough for remembering. The nature of classroom content requires focused attention. This means it requires effortful processing, and you must try to remember it. It is not automatically remembered. That means it requires your selective attention.

Attend

Attention is the next step. Once you sense, you must attend to the information. By choosing to pay attention to the information presented in class, you are giving your brain a chance to understand and encode that information for better understanding. This includes relating the content to other information you already know and, perhaps, relating it to other memories you have. But attention is a limited resource. We cannot pay attention to all things. In fact, from a cognitive perspective, you can only consciously attend to one source of information at a time. So, knowing this, limiting the amount of sources around you (cell phone, television, et cetera) that may attempt to steal your attention is necessary for efficient and effective learning.

All of this increases your chances of long-term retention, but in many cases, this is still not enough. For instance, I'll have students listen to the lecture and sincerely attend to the material presented. They will ask questions and indicate to me they have comprehended the information. Then, the next day during class, they struggle to answer questions at the beginning of class utilizing the content. The memory of yesterday's lesson is weak. It needs something to strengthen and increase the likelihood it can be used when required.

Rehearse

So, you've sensed the material. You've attended to the material. The next necessary step is rehearsal of that material. You've got to use it to remember it...most of the time. If you're not, you're taking a massive risk. Imagine, as an athlete learning a new formation or play during one practice session, never rehearsing it again, and being expected to use it flawlessly during a game. That would not be a good recipe for success on the playing field. Rehearsing information in the classroom works similarly and can take many different forms. It can look like answering a multiple-choice question, it can sound like a discussion, and it can even take the form of some sort of project. The important aspect is the material that needs to be accessed from your memory and used appropriately.

This is why I begin many lessons with retrieval of information from previous classes. It provides an opportunity for students to apply the concepts and terms in several different scenarios. Generally speaking, when a particular concept is retrieved from memory and rehearsed over a period of class meetings or study sessions (spaced practice), the memory is more likely to be "found" the next time the brain goes looking for it. Now, every teacher knows it would be pretty impossible to rehearse all content. Time is always of the essence in the classroom and what should be rehearsed and retrieved has to be prioritized. How I prioritize what my students rehearse in class is further discussed in Chapter 10.

So, to be certain, this isn't a comprehensive understanding of memory, but I do believe it provides an entry point for students and teachers alike to improve their classroom and/or studying. I can envision this information being packaged for a 30-minute professional development, a classroom poster, or maybe even a quick lesson in class. The great thing about this information is that it isn't content or age specific. Whether it's ten-year-olds in a science class or 17-year-olds in a language arts class, this information is valid and important for all learners and teachers to understand.

3 Choke Points
Attention

Let's take a look at the original image of memory processing.

Again, it provides you with a nice understanding of where and how memories progress from sensation to long-term memory. It would be wonderful if this process worked unencumbered while in school or while learning anything anywhere, but that is not the case. While the illustration is nice and neat, the real-world environment is often quite messy. There are mental and environmental hurdles along the memory processing path to trip us up. And, as important as it is to know and understand how we learn, it is also critical to understand where we fall short.

DOI: 10.4324/9781003472056-4

Learning material

↓

SENSES

↓

Sensory memory

↓

ATTENTION

Selection & focus

↕

Working memory

↕

Elaborative rehearsal

↓

Long-term memory

Dr. Stephen Chew wrote an incredibly accessible article discussing what he termed *choke points* and *pitfalls* of learning and memory.[1]

He defines *choke points* as "constraints in the human cognitive system" and *pitfalls* as "common traps students fall in that undermines their learning." He identifies four choke points and three pitfalls across the learning process. The next page shows the original image seen on the previous page with these choke points and pitfalls included. Now, this may seem like a lot of information...and it is. Do not be overwhelmed. The remainder of Part I explains these choke points and pitfalls extensively and discusses how to avoid them during instruction and the learning process.

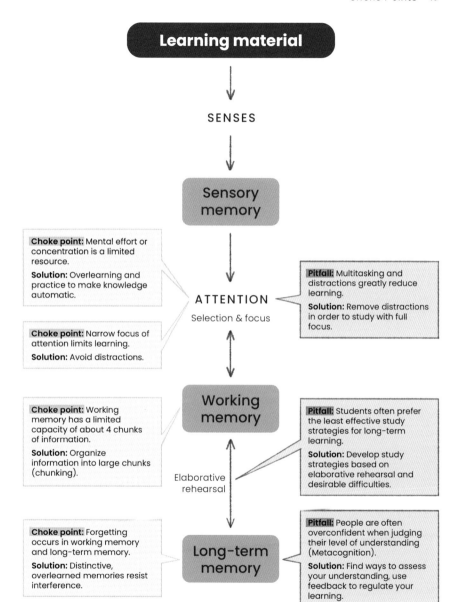

As you can see, there are many unfortunate opportunities for distraction and forgetting along the learning process. Understanding when and where they occur and how we can, to the best of our abilities, mitigate these choke points and pitfalls is a very important aspect of both designing instruction and creating a successful learning environment. As for the four choke points, there's no way to avoid them. Again, they are constraints and limitations on human memory. We can only learn to work within those boundaries. The three pitfalls are a little different. We can understand when and where we might experience them, as teachers and learners, and adjust our studies or environment accordingly to avoid them.

So, just as we worked our way from top to bottom when discussing the basic processes of memory, I think it fitting to do the same when looking at the choke points and pitfalls since this represents how and when different stimuli and/or experiences can hinder the learning process.

Learning material

↓

SENSES

↓

Sensory memory

↓

Choke point: Mental effort or concentration is a limited resource.

Solution: Overlearning and practice to make knowledge automatic.

Choke point: Narrow focus of attention limits learning.

Solution: Avoid distractions.

ATTENTION

Selection & focus

Pitfall: Multitasking and distractions greatly reduce learning.

Solution: Remove distractions in order to study with full focus.

Choke point: Working memory has a limited capacity of about 4 chunks of information.

Solution: Organize information into large chunks (chunking).

Working memory

Pitfall: Students often prefer the least effective study strategies for long-term learning.

Solution: Develop study strategies based on elaborative rehearsal and desirable difficulties.

Elaborative rehearsal

Choke point: Forgetting occurs in working memory and long-term memory.

Solution: Distinctive, overlearned memories resist interference.

Long-term memory

Pitfall: People are often overconfident when judging their level of understanding (Metacognition).

Solution: Find ways to assess your understanding, use feedback to regulate your learning.

Dr. Chew identifies two choke points and one pitfall at the stage of attention. There are no other singular phases in memory processing where there are more opportunities for learning to be stifled. Early in the processing of memory, there are already significant potential barriers to learning.

These choke points and pitfalls must be addressed. Assuming the to-be learned material is sensed, securing attention is (in my opinion) the largest barrier to learning I see in the classroom. And, as you might've guessed, if learning is derailed at this point, there's no chance to move forward in memory processing. So, with the remainder of this chapter, let's take a look at those first two choke points.

Learning material

↓

SENSES

↓

Sensory memory

↓

Choke point: Mental effort or concentration is a limited resource.
Solution: Overlearning and practice to make knowledge automatic.

Choke point: Narrow focus of attention limits learning.
Solution: Avoid distractions.

ATTENTION
Selection & focus

Pitfall: Multitasking and distractions greatly reduce learning.
Solution: Remove distractions in order to study with full focus.

Working memory

Choke point: Working memory has a limited capacity of about 4 chunks of information.
Solution: Organize information into large chunks (chunking).

Pitfall: Students often prefer the least effective study strategies for long-term learning.
Solution: Develop study strategies based on elaborative rehearsal and desirable difficulties.

Elaborative rehearsal

↓

Choke point: Forgetting occurs in working memory and long-term memory.
Solution: Distinctive, overlearned memories resist interference.

Long-term memory

Pitfall: People are often overconfident when judging their level of understanding (Metacognition).
Solution: Find ways to assess your understanding, use feedback to regulate your learning.

CHOKE POINT 1 - MENTAL EFFORT OR CONCENTRATION IS A LIMITED RESOURCE

This is a big one and brings to light another important topic to touch on to better understand learning capabilities in the classroom. We only have so much concentration and mental "space" for understanding material at any time. Different aspects of the learning environment and the material to be learned impose a kind of "load" on our conscious mind. This is part of what is called cognitive load theory (CLT).[2] While this theory is not the main focus of this book, it is incredibly important to have a basic understanding of CLT.

Cognitive Load Theory

Below is a quick overview of what is a quite intricate concept. According to cognitive load theory, within the task of learning anything, there are types of loads imposed on the process of memory (specifically working memory):

1) *Intrinsic Load* - the load caused by the complexity of the material

2) *Extraneous Load* - the load caused by how the material is presented[3]

Expanding on these definitions, *intrinsic load* relates to the nature of the content. Some content is quite simple and, therefore, imposes a relatively low load. Other content is more complex and requires a greater amount of background knowledge within a domain to understand without overloading working memory. For instance, learning a new term in a class imposes a low amount of intrinsic load; know term, know definition, understand how it is applied. But with a complex process, like the workings of the sodium/potassium pump to help maintain osmotic equilibrium...intrinsic load is much higher. The amount of information that needs to be understood and held in working memory simultaneously is greater, and instruction should be adjusted accordingly.

Intrinsic load is inherent in learning. There must be information to learn, and therefore, there must be a level of complexity associated with that material. A worthwhile concept to further understand here is element interactivity. Elements are anything that needs to be processed or learned. The greater the number of elements that need to be processed at any one time, to understand a concept or process, increases element interactivity. When novice learners have very little background knowledge of a particular concept or schema, element interactivity may very quickly overwhelm working memory (remember from earlier, information that cannot be chunked due to a lack of background knowledge more quickly "fill" the limited capacity of working memory). However, when students are simply adding to already well-established schemas, element activity is much less severe, leaving more "room" in working memory for extraneous load.[4]

Extraneous load relates to the instructional strategies used to disseminate the material to the learners. How we present information, or how students encounter the content, matters and imposes a load on the learner's working memory in addition to the intrinsic load. Utilizing methods in class to instruct that have many parts or intricate instructions to follow imposes its own extraneous load on the learner's memory. The more complex the methods, the greater the extraneous load. The greater the extraneous load, the less room for intrinsic load.

For instance, general instructions to read a particular passage and answer questions 1-5 are simple, easy to remember, and, therefore, elicit a low amount of extraneous load, leaving more room for students to focus on the to-be remembered information from the text. However, if students are completing a complicated project or sequence of events to utilize material, requiring students to remember all of the steps to complete the project successfully necessitates a higher extraneous load and leaves less room for the intrinsic load of the actual material.

Cognitive Overload

What needs to be avoided in class is termed cognitive overload. This occurs when the intrinsic load and the extraneous load, together, create a situation where the demands placed on a person's working memory exceed their ability to process information. When this occurs, learning and remembering are impeded upon and compromised. Usually, this results in either the student forgetting necessary instructions (extraneous load) or not focusing on the actual content (intrinsic load) and not remembering that information. Generally speaking, the more complicated the material (higher intrinsic load), the simpler the method of instruction (extraneous load) needed. Doing this creates a scenario where students are less likely to experience cognitive overload and more successfully process content.

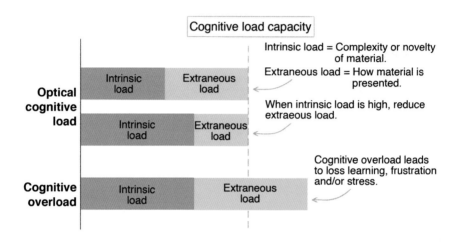

By providing a simple explanation of cognitive load theory, I hope choke point 1 is better understood. Mental effort is a limited resource. While working from sensory memory to long-term memory, students only have so much "room" to give. Specifically, within the confines of attention and working memory, the complexity of the material and the instructional strategies used need to be taken into consideration to more appropriately design an efficient and effective learning environment.

CHOKE POINT 2 - NARROW FOCUS OF ATTENTION LIMITS MEMORY

The ability to attend is quite limited. We can only attend consciously to one specific stimuli at any time. This is called selective attention. Quite literally, we either consciously or unconsciously select what we will attend to within our environment. By doing so, we are giving ourselves a chance to continue with memory processing.

However, by selecting one stimulus to attend to, we are conversely deciding to not attend to the myriad of other stimuli within the environment. Obviously, this choke point really constricts memory processing. Would humans be much more effective at remembering information if they could possibly consciously attend to multiple stimuli? Of course. And that would vastly change just about everything we know about memory. Alas, that is not the case. Both teachers and learners benefit from understanding this limitation of memory, though. It should influence how we design the classroom, instruction, and the conversations we have with students about more efficient learning.

While there are many other texts that center on cognitive psychology and memory in education, there seems to be a void focusing extensively on attention in the classroom. As was covered in the previous chapter, all aspects of memory processing are important and necessary. The way I see it though, as a classroom teacher of nearly 20 years, attention may be the most impacted by the learner, teacher, instructional design, and environment. All of these variables have the ability to influence each other to varying degrees and, ultimately, either improve learning or make it nearly impossible.

So, as a reminder, attention occurs quite early in the memory process. Immediately after the information is sensed, we are mostly in control of what we attend to. And, what we attend to, we have a chance of further processing in memory. What we do not attend to is fading away within seconds. But it isn't always easy to select what to attend to. We are constantly inundated with sensation; about 11 million bits of information every second...and we can only consciously process about 40.[5]

The Battle for Attention

To provide a concrete example, at this very moment millions of light waves are entering your eyes. You cannot possibly attend to all of them. You are, hopefully, deciding to attend to the waves that are creating these words on this page. Because of that conscious decision, you cannot also attend to the light waves in your peripheral vision. That information, while still being processed in the retina and ultimately in the occipital lobes of the brain, will never be remembered due to your lack of attention to it. And so it is with all of our senses. We choose how to spend our limited attention. All other sensation is forgotten in mere seconds.

It becomes more complicated, however, when we begin to understand that our senses interact and one can interfere with another's ability to be attended to. For instance, while your eyes and conscious attention are focusing on the words on this page, you are not consciously aware of the sound of the air conditioner in the room...but, if like most, you are now focused on the sound of the air conditioner (or any other background noise), you cannot also be consciously attending to these words on the page. In this example, auditory stimuli are hindering your conscious processing of visual stimuli. Are you still sensing visually? Of course, but that does not imply you are selecting to consciously attend to that stimulus.

Attention Distractors

Once explained, this all seems quite logical. But, students (and teachers) don't intuitively understand this, and they certainly don't apply it to their learning environment or instruction in the classroom without sincere effort. There are so many distractions in the classroom; from technology to peers to classroom decorations and layout. And it only takes one stimulus to steal our limited attention...one errant sound, one vibration of a cell phone, one captivating, but irrelevant, visual. This may result in missing valuable material and hindering learning for not only one student, but those around them. The more I think about it, it's almost a wonder we're able to relay any information to students and have them remember it. There seems to be an uphill battle over attention in the classroom.

Unfortunately, it also seems that a lot of what teachers are being asked to incorporate in the classroom and how they are being told to teach sometimes goes against what we know about memory processing and cognitive architecture. We will look at three possible areas of attention stealing: technology, peers, and the teacher. All, by themselves, are enough to be detrimental to a learning environment...but put them together and our limited attention to instruction is greatly hampered. It is incredibly important for teachers to understand where these thieves of attention arise and how to mitigate their negative impact on learning.

Technology as a Distractor

Is there a greater, more ubiquitous, distraction in the classroom right now than technology? On a daily basis, I know I battle cell phones and smart watches and laptops. I'm sure you do, too. For all their value, and I do believe laptops and cell phones can be used for learning purposes, they tend to be more of a hindrance to learning than anything else. It has become too easy to selectively attend to a screen in the classroom or to respond to the buzz of a cell phone. And, as we now know, when you attend to one stimulus in an environment, you are simultaneously choosing to not attend to any other stimuli that require conscious effort to process and remember. Even when students believe they can multi-task and pay attention to both their social media and the lesson at hand, they are sadly mistaken (more on this with Pitfall 1).

Laptops and cell phones are chief examples of technology in the classroom that can be used in an advantageous manner for learning, but also pose a big possible distraction for students. A study at the University of Michigan looking at student perceptions of how laptops affect their attentiveness, engagement, and learning surveyed students from 16 different courses that allow laptop use.[6] Seventy-five percent of students reported using a laptop increased the amount of time they spent on non-course tasks (35% said they spent more than ten minutes per class using social networking sites and email) and around 40% reported feeling somewhat or significantly distracted by students seated near them using a laptop. One student said the following, "Laptops do help with taking notes a lot and with being able to look at PowerPoints on the computer and add your own notes...However, they are also distracting because you end up on Facebook when you think the lecture is at a point you don't need to pay attention."

This is a really interesting statement from the student. Essentially, it involves a student assessing the importance of learning material, assigning a value to it, and then deciding whether it is worth their time to attend to that material. While I really appreciate a student thinking about the material being presented, I'm not sure they will have the best understanding of how important a particular slide or activity is during instruction. While a few minutes of a lesson may be judged to be boring by a student, do they recognize how important that content may be in comprehending the next step in a concept? This is problematic for many reasons and I wonder if students consciously understand they are making these sorts of potentially detrimental decisions about instruction when they do so. There is some research to indicate they don't. A different study found that even when students know of the negative influence device use during class may have on learning, they downplay the impact and report that their use of a digital device leads to little or no effect.[7]

Another study out of Canada found similar findings with respect to distractibility of information and communication technologies (ICTs) in the classroom.[8] Seventy-six percent acknowledged distraction as a negative effect of using and/or having ICTs during lecture, and 48.6% said other students' ICT use negatively impacted their ability to attend to class. When asked specifically how they used their ICT for non-academic purposes, the most reported uses were checking email and instant messaging (both at 70.7%), reading or posting on social media websites (49.8%), looking up words or definitions or trying to clarify information (44.3%), and completing work for other classes (33.8%). This study also asked participants when they were most likely to engage in non-academic activities with their ICT. The most frequent responses were during the break period (86.1%), whenever they felt they would not miss new content (58.5%), and whenever they were bored (37.6%).

Very clearly, even if intended to be used by students for academic purposes, cell phones and laptops steal attention and lead to distraction from classroom instruction. And it certainly isn't as if these distractions are harmless. Many studies indicate the detrimental cost on learning. Ravizza, Uitvlugt, and Fenn[9] observed that students spent nearly 37 minutes per class browsing the internet for non-academic purposes. A negative correlation was observed in this study with respect to non-academic internet use and final-exam score.

Another study, whose primary purpose was to examine the relationship between laptop use and student learning, found that laptop use was "significantly and negatively related to student learning." Interestingly enough, student surveys also reported a negative correlation between the level of laptop use and how clear students found the lessons and how well they believed they understood the course material.[10]

However you slice it, when ICT usage is not strictly monitored, students will often choose to selectively attend to their devices in the classroom when left to their own devices. And this will have a negative impact on student learning.

Peers as a Distractor

Sometimes I'll hear from students that their actions in class only impact their learning, so why should it bother me if they want to be off task? Well, as you might have guessed, students in class distract each other. Even if it isn't some major incident and a student is quietly off task, that can influence how much their peers attend to the lesson.

Attention Contagion

The term for this phenomenon is *attention contagion*. Essentially, if a student is surrounded by peers displaying inattentive behaviors, those inattentive actions are contagious. Interestingly enough, if a student is surrounded by peers displaying attentive behaviors, those actions are also contagious.

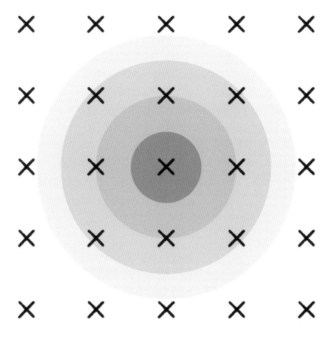

One study had participants (undergraduate students) observe a lecture with a confederate of the study.[11] A confederate is someone who aids the experimenter by posing as a participant, but whose behavior is rehearsed prior to the experiment. The confederate would either display attentive behaviors (leaning forward, taking notes, et cetera) or inattentive behaviors (slouching, shifting gaze, glancing at the clock, taking infrequent notes, et cetera). Researchers watched the participant to see if they were more or less likely to imitate the confederates' behaviors. Researchers also instructed the confederates to not add distraction to the environment via visual or auditory stimuli. They wanted to ensure the confederates' inattentive behavior would be less active and engaging. In experiment 1 of this study, the participants being studied were seated behind either an attentive or inattentive confederate. After watching a video of a lecture, participants completed surveys, and a multiple-choice question quiz on the topics covered during the video was administered. Here are some of the results:

1) Participants were asked, on a scale of 1–10, to rate the attentiveness of the other person (the confederate) in the room. Interestingly enough, it appears that the participants were able to distinguish between attentive and inattentive behavior because the average rating for attentive confederates was 8.88 and 4.29 for inattentive confederates.

2) Participants rated inattentive confederates as being more distracting than those with attentive confederates in the room.

3) Participants in rooms with attentive confederates took significantly more notes during the lecture and rated themselves as being on task more than those with inattentive confederates.

4) When analyzing the results of the multiple-choice quiz, those participants with attentive confederates scored better (58.75 average) than those with inattentive confederates (53.14 average).

In experiment 2 of this study, researchers manipulated conditions in one significant manner: this time through the lecture, the participants would be seated in front of the confederates. They did this to really test the boundaries of the contagiousness of either the attentive or inattentive confederate. The main research question seeking to be answered in experiment 2 was as follows: *can students "catch" the (in)attentive states of peers who are not visible to them?* It's one thing to see a peer in class not paying attention and deciding that the material might not be important. It is another thing entirely to not be able to sense, visually, the inattentive peer and still have that impact on a student's actions. Some of the results for experiment 2 are as follows:

1) Participants were significantly more attentive when paired with attentive confederates. Participants were less fidgety and less sleepy.

2) Participants who watched the lecture with attentive confederates took slightly more notes than those with inattentive confederates.

3) Participants ratings of how distracting the confederates were were not significantly different between groups.

4) Participants with attentive confederates did score slightly better (55.86 average) than participants with inattentive confederates (53.67 average), though these scores are not statistically significant.

So, what do these results tell us? This research appears to show some level of attention contagion. Especially in experiment 1, participants were aware of the level of attentiveness of the other learner (the confederate) in the room, and this correlated with the participants level of attentiveness, number of notes taken, and their score on a quiz. Even in experiment 2, when the confederate was out of sight, participants were more attentive with attentive confederates, took more notes, and made slightly higher on the quiz.

What I find really interesting is that participants in experiment 2 did not consciously realize how distracting the confederate was and certainly did not feel the impact of this on their actions. Bottom line: attention is contagious. When peers in the classroom are more attentive, that impacts the attentiveness of others. It's a bit of a snowball effect, right? If more students begin to actively pay attention during class, other students will join in. But, unfortunately, it appears the opposite is also true. Teachers and learners need to know this and design the learning and/or studying environment appropriately.

Attention Contagion in the Online World

Researchers also found evidence of attention contagion in the world of online learning.[12] Participants (undergraduate students) watched a video lecture along with confederates who showed up in video thumbnails. Just like in the first experiment, some participants watched the video with attentive confederates and some with inattentive confederates. The results? Participants who watched with attentive confederates reported being more attentive and performed 12% better on a quiz after the lecture. Interestingly, these same participants also believed the lesson to be more important. As the researchers state, "Attention is contagious online."

Attention Contagion with ICT

And what happens when you place inattentive students with ICT usage in the learning environment? As you might have guessed...it's not good. One group of researchers conducted two experiments to analyze the impact of off-task laptop usage during a lecture on student learning.[13] In experiment 1, all participants were instructed to listen to the lecture and take notes on the laptop. Half of the participants were also assigned 12 random tasks to complete on the laptop during the lecture when they felt it to be convenient. A lot of the tasks asked participants to look up certain information via an internet search or any sort of task that might mimic legitimate off-task behavior on a laptop during class. The results reflect what you might imaging: participants who were assigned the off-task condition during the lecture scored, on average, 11% lower on the post lesson quiz than those who were not in that group.

In experiment 2, a few of the conditions were changed to see if those seated within view of those participants in the off-task condition were impacted by the ability to see those inattentive behaviors. Students were seated strategically throughout the classroom; some students were able to see the laptop screens of those off-task and some were not. After the lecture, all students completed a quiz on the content, and the scores were analyzed. The big finding? Participants in view of a peer with the off-task condition scored, on average, 17% lower than those students who were not able to see the off-task laptop behaviors.

Without a doubt, attentive and inattentive behaviors in the classroom (and online) are contagious and impact learning. Not only do we, as teachers, need to make the learning environment as distraction free as possible, we need to tell our students their actions impact others and they are impacted by the actions of others...whether they realize it or not.

The Teacher as a Distractor

It may seem a bit harsh to label the teacher, the one who is the biggest champion for learning in the classroom as a distractor, but it can be true. Although we always mean well, sometimes we don't necessarily design the classroom in a manner that is the most conducive for learning. And, sometimes, our instruction doesn't exactly line up with what we know about memory and attention, so there are some things to consider on that front. Ultimately, we want to do the best for our students to improve learning, so it is extremely advantageous to consider our craft, to be professional about what we do, and improve where we need to improve, for our students.

Classroom Environment

Consider the environment of your classroom. Think about the seating. Think about what's on the walls and what may be outside your windows (if you're lucky enough to have windows). Think about all of the external stimuli that can (and do) impact attention before, during, and after a lesson. It can be a lot to consider, and some of this can be outside our control. For instance, with respect to seating design, I am limited to tables. I am not the biggest fan of tables. I would much more prefer individual desks. I can place two desks together to make a table, but I cannot break a table in two to create two desks. And seating is incredibly important to consider with respect to student attention. As we've already seen, it does not take much to steal attention away from a lesson. Attention is contagious, and any small hurdle that gets in the way of a student selectively attending to the necessary material might be enough to stymie learning. So, in my classroom, I have no students seated with their backs turned to whomever is presenting the content. All students are facing the whiteboard and/or projection of the lesson. Just having to turn around to see and listen can be enough of a hindrance to stop a student from attending to the lesson.

I know it might not be the most fashionable in education right now to not provide flexible seating, but I find that those sorts of seating arrangements only lead to more easily distractable students. There are other ways to build relationships with students and make them feel more "at home" in the classroom that do not lead to distractions from learning.

What about decorations on the wall? Those need to be considered also. My general rule is that nothing needs to be on the wall that does not correspond with material being taught. Anything outside that can be a distraction to the student. If you want to put up motivational posters or examples of wonderful student work, that's fine, but maybe put them in the back of the room where students are not facing during the lesson.

I know that what I'm describing may seem like a "boring" classroom, but I've found that a classroom isn't boring because of where students sit or how many colorful posters I have on the wall. What I believe plays more of a determining factor in the motivation and amiability of students has to do with the engaging nature of the lesson and the success of the students. And it's really tough to be successful if students aren't paying attention. And it can be more difficult to pay attention if the classroom isn't designed with attention in mind. Attention creates student success, which, in turn, leads to greater student motivation. And a more motivated student is a more attentive student.

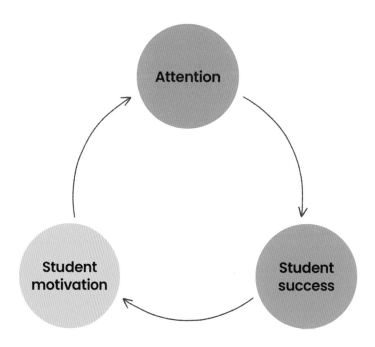

Classroom Instruction

Now let's take a greater look at how instruction is conducted. As with how the classroom is designed, instructional design can also impact attention in a negative manner. To begin, what are some behaviors by teachers that students notice during instruction that may distract or impede learning? A 2018 study asked just this question to undergraduate college-aged students.[14] They arranged their findings into three categories:

1) Incompetence/Indolence/Lecture – "When giving a power point, she tends to talk fast as well as change the slides fast. Like two minutes per slide with 500 words." There were 72 respondents who identified this as a distractor to learning in this study.

2) Offensive/Antagonism – "When the instructor said a vulgar word." There were five respondents who identified this as a distractor to learning in this study.

3) Classroom Management – "He played music in the background during a group project." There were seven respondents who identified this as a distractor to learning in this study.

As a teacher, I find these student-reported issues to be quite interesting. It is so important to not forget what it's like to be in a learning environment where any extra stimuli (like background music) may serve as a distraction or where a little extra time is needed to properly digest a wealth of information for understanding.

Cognitive Load Theory Effects

A last area of focus for teachers to consider when prioritizing student attention during instruction leads us back to cognitive load theory. Remember, there are aspects of a lesson that are inherent, like the material to be learned (intrinsic load). There are also aspects of a lesson that involve how the material is taught (extraneous load). Both are important and necessary, but too much of a combination of the two and students experience cognitive overload.

Sometimes, in how we present material, students experience unnecessary amounts of extraneous load. There are three effects to focus on here: the *seductive details effect*, the *split-attention effect*, and the *redundancy effect*. Once understood, these three effects are pretty easy to eliminate from instruction. But, until brought to light, they may have a detrimental impact on learning by steering attention away from the necessary material to be learned.

The Seductive Details Effect

Seductive details are "highly interesting and entertaining information that is only tangentially related to the topic but is irrelevant..."[15] That funny story you tell about the time your family went to the Grand Canyon or the cool GIF of rain you add to your slide about the water cycle... those are seductive details, and they don't necessarily add anything to the learning in your classroom. In fact, there's research to say that those irrelevant stimuli only add to distract and confuse students about the important content to be remembered from a lesson. When you include the picture of your family on vacation or that moving graphic, students may become attentive to the wrong information and either misremember necessary content or miss it all together.

One meta-analysis looked at many different studies on the topic and concluded that "including seductive details in learning material can hinder learning."[16] As a teacher, this reminds me to first and foremost focus on what is necessary for learning. If I am to add any extra personal touch to my lessons, it needs to be instrumental for understanding the information. Otherwise, students may remember the joke I told that is somewhat related to the material, but not remember the content. Believe me, this can be difficult. It seems second nature to personalize instruction...and if students want to do this from their own life, that is great and wonderful for learning. But, when they cannot directly relate to that story or if their attention is steered away from the important information for any reason, it can be detrimental to student learning and understanding. They may experience a rise in extraneous load leading to cognitive overload.

Split-Attention Effect

This effect "occurs when learners are required to split their attention between at least two sources of information that have been separated either spatially or temporally."[17] This may occur when a diagram is on one slide of a presentation and the text, which is necessary for understanding the diagram is on the next slide. It may also take place when the instructions for completing an assignment are explained at the beginning of a class period, but the activity doesn't actually begin for several minutes. "By requiring learners to integrate several sources of information that are separated in space or time, extraneous cognitive load is created."[18]

Most of the time, the split-attention effect is experienced with multimedia. So, whenever possible, teachers need to include all of the information necessary for learning or for completing an activity in a manner that doesn't require students to split their attention; include all of the necessary content on the graph, for example. Whenever students are required to go back and forth to access the necessary content, task switching can occur, and an unnecessary extraneous load (which could lead to cognitive overload) can hinder learning.

The Redundancy Effect

This effect "may occur when the multiple sources of information can be understood separately without the need for mental integration."[19] The redundancy effect basically says to not include information in different forms or modalities if it can be completely understood via one form.

For example, if a graph can be completely understood by the information included in the graph, there is no need to include additional text also explaining the information in the graph. Providing an additional explanation of something that has already been sufficiently explained once will not lead to more learning. In fact, it can be detrimental to the process by again overloading extraneous load. Learners may be wasting their time by reading or hearing the redundant information.

This may lead them to use limited working memory capacity to try and parcel out what is important and what is not, thereby missing other necessary information. Cognitive overload can certainly occur because of this. One of the most common examples in the classroom of the redundancy effect occurs when teachers speak the words that are also being presented on a slide. This forces students to try and experience and comprehend the material in multiple modalities (visually and auditorily). If both are not necessary, only one should be incorporated into instruction.

Taken individually, all three of these effects can have a negative impact on a student's ability to attend to the necessary material. Put them together in one lesson, and you've got several cognitive hurdles for students to attempt to navigate (sometimes unconsciously) to be successful. As teachers, to the best of our ability, we need to be aware of how we set up the classroom, how one student's actions can impact another's attention, and design instruction that best works within the confines of what we know about memory and attention. If we don't, we are sacrificing the efficiency and effectiveness of student learning.

Notes

1 Chew, S. L. (2021). An advance organizer for student learning: Choke points and pitfalls in studying. *Canadian Psychology/Psychologie Canadienne, 62*(4), 420.

2 Sweller, J., Ayres, P., & Kalyuga, S. (2011). *Cognitive load theory.* Springer.

3 Kalyuga, S. (2011). Cognitive load theory: How many types of load does it really need? *Educational Psychology Review, 23*, 1-19.

4 Sweller, J., Ayres, P., & Kalyuga, S. (2011). *Cognitive load theory.* Springer.

5 Wilson, T. D. (2004). *Strangers to ourselves: Discovering the adaptive unconscious.* Harvard University Press.

6 Zhu, E., Kaplan, M., Dershimer, R. C., & Bergom, I. (2011). Use of laptops in the classroom: Research and best practices. *CRLT Occasional Papers, 30*(6), 1-6.

7 Kirschner, P. A., & Karpinski, A. C. (2010). Facebook® and academic performance. *Computers in Human Behavior, 26*(6), 1237-1245.

8 Vahedi, Z., Zannella, L., & Want, S. C. (2021). Students' use of information and communication technologies in the classroom: Uses, restriction, and integration. *Active Learning in Higher Education*, *22*(3), 215–228.

9 Ravizza, S. M., Uitvlugt, M. G., & Fenn, K. M. (2017). Logged in and zoned out: How laptop internet use relates to classroom learning. *Psychological Science*, *28*(2), 171–180.

10 Fried, C. B. (2008). In-class laptop use and its effects on student learning. *Computers & Education*, *50*(3), 906–914.

11 Forrin, N. D., Huynh, A. C., Smith, A. C., Cyr, E. N., McLean, D. B., Siklos-Whillans, J., Risko, E. F., Smilek, D., & MacLeod, C. M. (2021). Attention spreads between students in a learning environment. *Journal of Experimental Psychology: Applied*, *27*(2), 276.

12 Kalsi, S. S., Forrin, N. D., Sana, F., MacLeod, C. M., & Kim, J. A. (2023). Attention contagion online: Attention spreads between students in a virtual classroom. *Journal of Applied Research in Memory and Cognition*, *12*(1), 59.

13 Sana, F., Weston, T., & Cepeda, N. J. (2013). Laptop multitasking hinders classroom learning for both users and nearby peers. *Computers & Education*, *62*, 24–31.

14 Frisby, B. N., Sexton, B. T., Buckner, M. M., Beck, A. C., & Kaufmann, R. (2018). Peers and instructors as sources of distraction from a cognitive load perspective. *International Journal for the Scholarship of Teaching and Learning*, *12*(2), 6.

15 Harp, S. F., & Mayer, R. E. (1998). How seductive details do their damage: A theory of cognitive interest in science learning. *Journal of Educational Psychology*, *90*(3), 414.

16 Sundararajan, N., & Adesope, O. (2020). Keep it coherent: A meta-analysis of the seductive details effect. *Educational Psychology Review*, *32*(3), 707–734.

17 Sweller, J., Ayres, P., & Kalyuga, S. (2011). *Cognitive load theory*. Springer. p. 111.

18 Sweller, J., Ayres, P., & Kalyuga, S. (2011). *Cognitive load theory*. Springer. p. 111.

19 Sweller, J., Ayres, P., & Kalyuga, S. (2011). *Cognitive load theory*. Springer. p. 141.

4 Pitfall
Multitasking

PITFALL 1 – MULTITASKING AND DISTRACTIONS GREATLY REDUCE LEARNING

One of the most crucial mistakes people make when learning is an attempt at multitasking. Multitasking is an incredibly common occurrence in the life of anyone who is, well, human. As a father, husband, and teacher, I can easily see examples in my life where I need to complete multiple tasks to get out the door on time or be prepared for class. We believe by completing two things at once, we are saving time...but we're usually not. This is especially true if the two tasks both require conscious effort and attention to successfully complete.

The Myth of Multitasking

Similarly, in the classroom or any setting where people are studying, learners believe they can multitask in a number of ways and still efficiently and effectively learn the to-be-remembered material. You may have even heard students proclaim they are good at multitasking; boasting how they can watch Netflix while also reading their notes or listen to music while also attending to a lecture. However, whether they believe they are good at multitasking or not...they're not. "What is clear is that people are not capable of thinking two different thoughts at the same time."[1] The brain, as remarkable as it truly is, certainly has its limitations...and this is one of them.

DOI: 10.4324/9781003472056-5

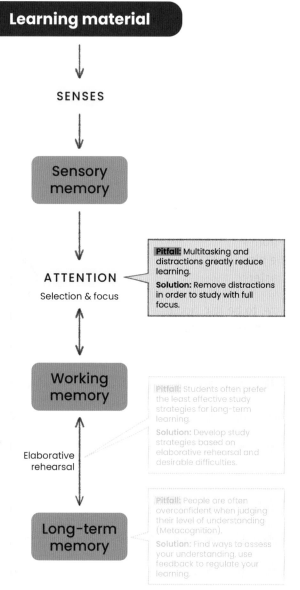

Choke point: Mental effort or concentration is a limited resource.
Solution: Overlearning and practice to make knowledge automatic.

Choke point: Narrow focus of attention limits learning.
Solution: Avoid distractions.

Choke point: Working memory has a limited capacity of about 4 chunks of information.
Solution: Organize information into large chunks (chunking).

Choke point: Forgetting occurs in working memory and long-term memory.
Solution: Distinctive, overlearned memories resist interference.

Pitfall: Multitasking and distractions greatly reduce learning.
Solution: Remove distractions in order to study with full focus.

Pitfall: Students often prefer the least effective study strategies for long-term learning.
Solution: Develop study strategies based on elaborative rehearsal and desirable difficulties.

Pitfall: People are often overconfident when judging their level of understanding (Metacognition).
Solution: Find ways to assess your understanding, use feedback to regulate your learning.

Not too long ago, I helped my son shed the training wheels and learn to ride his bicycle on his own. This is a demanding task. From a cognitive perspective, the rider has to attempt to focus on two tasks at once, pedaling with their feet to keep the bike moving and steering with the handlebars to avoid running into anything. Knowing this, while watching my son, you could witness the inability to do both of these at the same time as both of these tasks required his conscious attention. Whenever he focused on pedaling, his steering became much more erratic. Whenever he focused on steering, he would often forget to pedal at all. This resulted in him sometimes just falling over and sometimes running into objects that were right in front of him. There's no telling how many times he ran right into our back fence. But eventually, he got it. Essentially, what happened with practice is that one of those tasks became automatic. And, once he no longer had to direct attention to pedaling the bicycle, he could devote his full attention to steering. Once that was mastered, he was a full-fledged bike rider.

Now, to be fair, riding a bike is not the same as attempting to multitask in school. The muscle memory of riding, while at first is effortful, can become automatic with practice. This is not possible with knowledge acquired in school and while studying. If a student needed to complete both their English and math homework and decided to try to work on both at the same time, the results would be terrible. And, even if the student continually practiced this multitasking of coursework, they would never be successful at making it automatic. Again, this type of information (explicit memories) is a cognitively effortful process.

Usually, when I mention this in class, students bring up an example like "I can walk and talk at the same time. That's doing two things at once." While that is (hopefully) true, walking quickly becomes an automatic action in early childhood and requires no conscious attention. So, they really aren't completing two cognitively demanding tasks at once. A better example might be to ask students to calculate 37×14 on paper while, at the same time, reciting the Preamble to the U.S. Constitution. It becomes obvious, very quickly, that this cannot be done simultaneously. They may be able to complete both tasks, but it will not be concurrently.

Task Switching

What is really happening in situations such as the one mentioned above isn't actually multitasking. Cognitively, students are going back and forth between the two tasks requiring conscious consideration. It's called *task switching*, and there's a cost associated with that method of working through problems, too.

To easily show the time loss associated with task switching, I would like you to take part in a quick demonstration. This is also something you can easily incorporate into your classroom to show your students. You need a pen or pencil, a sheet of paper, and a timer of some sort. Here are your directions:

1) Time yourself as you first count from one to twenty-six. Record that time on your paper.
2) Time yourself as you recite the alphabet from A to Z. Record that time on your paper.
3) Time yourself switching back and forth between counting from one to twenty-six and reciting the alphabet from A to Z (A, 1, B, 2, C, 3...). Record that time.

Now, add up the times of tasks one and two. Compare that to the time of task three. There is a very high probability you spent less time first counting to twenty-six and then reciting the alphabet than when you alternated between the two tasks. And this only involved completing two tasks that have relatively low amounts of cognitive effort and with very little at stake from a learning perspective. Imagine if your students were attempting to task switch between two assignments that required much more effort to understand and learn. The ramifications would be dire, and learning would suffer immensely.

The activity above was actually devised by Dr. Yana Weinstein, a former professor and cognitive psychologist. She also used it in her classes to demonstrate the unfavorable impact of task switching.[2] And, while she used this with her college-aged students, I can easily see these results also applying to early years through college-aged learners, too. When she ran this quasi-experiment in her college courses, every single student took much longer to complete task three than task one and task two combined. The results can be seen on the chart below.

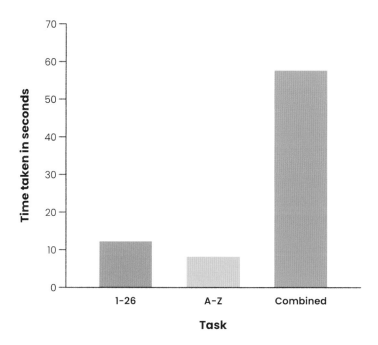

Every student experienced the inefficient impact of task switching. Again, this would be a wonderful activity to use in class to demonstrate why, when we are attempting to learn, we should not provide opportunities to switch tasks from studying our notes or reading to watching a few seconds of a Netflix show. The classroom discussion that could grow from this activity could really make an impact on the long-term methods of studying students choose to employ.

Task Switching's Negative Impact on Memory

To make matter worse, task switching isn't just inefficient; it doesn't just take longer to complete the tasks. There's also a negative effect on memory processing. When switching from one task to another, there is, at least, a few moments where other stimuli provide interference. This has been shown to lower memory performance on tasks.[3] Interestingly enough, when researchers developed a study where participants were asked to switch between a task with task-relevant information to another task with task-irrelevant information, their later memory recognition was lower for the task-relevant information and actually higher for the task-irrelevant information. It seems the brain may struggle, during task switching, to understand what is important to remember and what is immaterial.

In another experiment, participants were asked to either switch between tasks that were similar in topic or different. The participants who, when task switching, were required to remember information for different subjects performed poorer on a final task than those who switched between similar-subject tasks.[4] This certainly has further implications for attempts at task switching between course work and Netflix or notifications on their phone.

It is somewhat apparent, to combat this pitfall, students and teachers should study and learn with fewer distractions[5] and simplify the learning environment. Any stimuli that can either steal attention or elicit an attempt at multitasking is a deterrent to the learning process and should be eliminated.

Early in the memory process, there are already several hurdles to learning. Moving into working memory, Dr. Chew identifies another choke point that is vital for teachers and learners to consider that is incredibly important to when designing instruction and the learning environment.

Notes

1 Bruyckere, P. D., Kirschner, P. A., & Hulshof, C. D. (2015). *Urban myths about learning and education*. Academic Press.

2 Weinstein, Y. (2018, July 28). *The cost of task switching: A simply yet very powerful demonstration*. The Learning Scientists. https://www.learningscientists. org/blog/2017/7/28-1?rq=task%20switching

3 Richter, F. R., & Yeung, N. (2012). Memory and cognitive control in task switch-ing. *Psychological Science*, *23*(10), 1256–1263.

4 Muhmenthaler, M. C., & Meier, B. (2019). Task switching hurts memory encod-ing. *Experimental Psychology*, *66*(1), 58–67.

5 Ent, M. R., Baumeister, R. F., & Tice, D. M. (2015). Trait self-control and the avoidance of temptation. *Personality and Individual Differences*, *74*, 12–15.

5 Choke Points and Pitfalls
Working Memory

As was stated in earlier chapters, working memory has limitations in capacity. We can only consciously hold about four chunks of information in our working memory at any time. And, remember, whatever is in our working memory is what we are consciously considering. Knowing this, instruction and the learning environment should be designed to work within this constraint.

Chunking Information

One way to do this is to chunk information. By placing related information together (chunking the material), the differing elements can occupy a smaller space in working memory. Prior learning and background knowledge vastly impact a learner's ability to chunk information. Logically, it makes sense that you cannot chunk like material if you have no knowledge of related material. Seeing this through the lens of cognitive load theory, chunked information necessitates a lower impact on intrinsic load (the complexity of the material). When we already have some knowledge about a topic, any related material will be less complex in nature and be easier to add to the already created spider web of knowledge. Conversely, learners with lower background knowledge are limited

DOI: 10.4324/9781003472056-6

Learning material

SENSES

Sensory memory

Choke point: Mental effort or concentration is a limited resource.

Solution: Overlearning and practice to make knowledge automatic.

Choke point: Narrow focus of attention limits learning.

Solution: Avoid distractions.

ATTENTION
selective focusing

Pitfall: Multitasking and distractions greatly reduce learning.

Solution: Remove distractions in order to study with full focus.

Working memory

Choke point: Working memory has a limited capacity of about 4 chunks of information.

Solution: Organize information into large chunks (chunking).

Pitfall: Students often prefer ineffective study strategies for long-term learning.

Solution: Develop study strategies based on elaborative rehearsal and desirable difficulties.

elaborative rehearsal

Choke point: Forgetting occurs in working memory and long-term memory.

Solution: Distinctive, overlearned memories resist interference.

Long-term memory

Pitfall: People are often overconfident when judging their level of understanding (metacognition).

Solution: Find ways to assess your understanding, use feedback to regulate your learning.

in their ability to chunk information and will experience higher element interactivity in working memory.[1] This makes learning more complex material much more difficult and necessitates a change in how students should initially interact with this new material.

A more applicable example of the benefits of chunking in the classroom involves the use of mnemonics. At some point in my early years science classes, I needed to know the colors of the rainbow. The way I remember it, there are seven colors; red, orange, yellow, green, blue, indigo, and violet. On their own, there are seven elements to remember. That creates quite the load for working memory. Luckily, though, this load was lightened by the mnemonic Roy G. Biv, with each letter representing a color of the rainbow. Now, instead of remembering seven seemingly unrelated elements, I just have one to access, which chunks all of the necessary information.

These sorts of strategies, while well known, are often underutilized. I think we take them for granted and don't understand their value. With content that has a high number of elements, I will often ask my students to come up with silly sayings or mnemonics to help them remember the information and free up some of that limited capacity working memory and to ease the process of remembering the content.

Learning material

SENSES

Sensory memory

Choke point: Mental effort or concentration is a limited resource.

Solution: Overlearning and practice to make knowledge automatic.

ATTENTION

Choke point: Narrow focus of attention limits learning.

Solution: Avoid distractions.

Pitfall: Multitasking and distractions greatly reduce learning.

Solution: Remove distractions in order to study with full focus.

Working memory

Choke point: Working memory has a limited capacity of about 4 chunks of information.

Solution: Organize information into large chunks (chunking).

Elaborative rehearsal

Pitfall: Students often prefer the least effective study strategies for long-term learning.

Solution: Develop study strategies based on elaborative rehearsal and desirable difficulties.

Choke point: Forgetting occurs in working memory and long-term memory.

Solution: Distinctive, overlearned memories resist interference.

Long-term memory

Pitfall: People are often overconfident when judging their level of understanding (Metacognition).

Solution: Find ways to assess your understanding, use feedback to regulate your learning.

PITFALL 2 – STUDENTS OFTEN PREFER THE LEAST EFFECTIVE STUDY STRATEGIES FOR LONG-TERM LEARNING

Elaborate rehearsal of information is crucial for strengthening information and connections; retrieving memories stored in long-term memory and consciously recalling them in working memory. The more distributed, or spaced, these retrieval attempts are with particular content, the more efficient and effective we become at accessing those schemas of information (Part II further elaborates on these learning strategies).

The problem, though, is students may choose to rehearse when preparing for an assessment or for assessing their level of understanding, but they often seem to leave out the elaborative aspect. Most students do not choose the most advantageous methods for studying and maximizing the processing of material into long-term memory. And it's not really their fault. They are only modeling what they've been told to do. A surprisingly low number of my students, when asked, have ever had a teacher overtly discuss with them how to study. They just say "study." But studying isn't intuitive. It must be taught.

Often, students don't realize all studying is not created equal. The cognitively easier a method of study is, the easier the material to-be studied will probably be forgotten. This is something I say to my students a lot when talking about how they should study. Rereading your notes or the textbook may sound like a beneficial practice, and students may see immediate incremental gains, but they are fleeting. And most students see rereading as a "safe" option for studying. It feels good to read your notes and be reminded of what you know. There's no risk involved that you may not know the information or have additional content to look back over. Students just read through their notes and feel like "yep, I remembered all of that" and they're done. That "oh yeah, I remember that" sentiment feels like studying, but it really is not.

The information may be remembered for a few minutes, but in the long term, it is much more likely to be forgotten when assessed. The chances of that knowledge being accessible when it is needed (perhaps on an assessment of some kind) are quite low. Generally speaking, more cognitively effortful interactions with the information during studying creates longer lasting memories of content.

Retrieval Practice

When we speak of more elaborate and effortful rehearsal of material, we are speaking of *retrieval practice* (it is also called *the testing effect* in research literature).[2] Quite simply, this strategy involves learners retrieving information from their memory. With over a century of research to support this strategy, it is quite clear retrieval practice is one of, if not the most, beneficial learning and studying strategies in a variety of situations.[3] In addition, there is evidence of its effectiveness from the preschool aged through those aged over 50[4] and with learners of varying ability levels.[5]

There are numerous manners in which this can be done, but all create a situation where the student must use their brain to either recognize or recall information and use it appropriately. Even if this is just answering multiple choice questions, students must access memories to recognize the correct option among distractors. Simple recognition of information provides a more fruitful opportunity for learning and remembering than rereading a text or highlighting notes.

Spaced Practice

Another study strategy students rarely take advantage of that has a mountain of evidence pointing to its positive impact is *spaced practice* (it is also sometimes called *distributed practice* in research literature). As far back as the 1800s, researchers have been studying the effectiveness of spaced practice[6] and, again, have found positive results from the preschool level to those aged over 50.

Also, experiments have demonstrated advantageous results on a wide range of learning activities.[7] Spacing out retrieval of material is in contrast to a more commonly applied study method, cramming or massed practice. And, while massed practice may support short-term performance, spacing out retrieval opportunities supports long-term retention of material.[8]

Students erroneously believe they have successfully studied after rereading their notes, even if that really provides no accurate representation of their ability level and leads to false beliefs about their learning. So, when they choose to cram for a test the night before, they believe they're doing what they're supposed to do. Chances are, though, the next day or whenever they need to use that information, it will be inaccessible to them.

Even in some experimental settings, participants' judgement of learning is higher after cramming than for distributing their practice before an assessment.[9] Another study produced further results demonstrating poor decision-making on the part of learners when considering when to study. Only 11% of 472 college students questioned reported they plan their study schedule ahead of time.[10] That's not very good...at all.

It is understandable that planning ahead for studying can be difficult at any age, sometimes leaving the only option of massed practice for those who even attempt to study for assessments. But it is necessary to discuss and model in class to students that spacing retrieval practice of material is much more advantageous.

As mentioned earlier, many times the reason they don't use more effective methods of study is due to their not knowing any better. They're only doing what they've been taught or what they've seen their peers do. I know, in my psychology classes over the past decade, whenever we discuss cognitive psychology and topics like learning, memory, and study methods, an incredibly low percentage of students (I would guess very close to 0%) have ever heard of retrieval practice or spaced practice. I can't feasibly expect students to learn these more efficient and effective strategies if I don't teach them. The usage of retrieval practice and spaced practice will be greatly discussed in Part II of this book, along with many conversations I have with my students surrounding these topics.

Notes

1 Sweller, J., Ayres, P., & Kalyuga, S. (2011). *Cognitive load theory*. Springer.

2 Karpicke, J. D., & Roediger III, H. L. (2008). The critical importance of retrieval for learning. *Science, 319*(5865), 966–968.

3 Roediger, H. L., & Butler, A. C. (2011). The critical role of retrieval practice in long-term retention. *Trends in Cognitive Sciences, 15*(1), 20–27.

4 Carpenter, S. K., Pan, S. C., & Butler, A. C. (2022). The science of effective learning: Spacing, retrieval practice, and metacognition of strategy use. *Nature Reviews Psychology*.

5 Agarwal, P. K., Finley, J. R., Rose, N. S., & Roediger III, H. L. (2017). Benefits from retrieval practice are greater for students with lower working memory capacity. *Memory, 25*(6), 764–771.

6 Cepeda, N. J., Pashler, H., Vul, E., Wixted, J. T., & Rohrer, D. (2006). Distributed practice in verbal recall tasks: A review and quantitative synthesis. *Psychological Bulletin, 132*(3), 354.

7 Carpenter, S. K., Pan, S. C., & Butler, A. C. (2022). The science of effective learning: Spacing, retrieval practice, and metacognition of strategy use. *Nature Reviews Psychology*.

8 Bjork, R. A. (2017). *Creating desirable difficulties to enhance learning*. Crown House Publishing.

9 Simon, D. A., & Bjork, R. A. (2001). Metacognition in motor learning. *Journal of Experimental Psychology: Learning, Memory, and Cognition, 27*(4), 907.

10 Kornell, N., & Bjork, R. A. (2007). The promise and perils of self-regulated study. *Psychonomic Bulletin & Review, 14*(2), 219–224.

6 Choke Points and Pitfalls

Long-Term Memory

PITFALL 3 - PEOPLE ARE OFTEN OVERCONFIDENT WHEN JUDGING THEIR LEVEL OF UNDERSTANDING

Here's a common occurrence I've seen in the classroom: students enter the classroom and have some sort of assessment of material from a previous lesson or lessons. They complete the work and await the teacher providing feedback and the correct answers. A majority of students initially did not answer all of the questions correctly, but filled in the correct answers along the way with the teacher's discussion of the material. At the end of the activity, students are left believing they know the material because they ended up having all of the answers...even if they only have all questions answered correctly because the teacher told them the answers. This scenario, and others like it, perfectly illustrates pitfall three - overconfidence.

Generally speaking, students are quite poor at judging their level of understanding. They frequently believe they know material that they have not mastered because of the inefficient and ineffective study methods they use (Pitfall 2). In their mind, once they've encountered the information in class via presentation or collaborative work, they've got it. Or, once they've reread their notes during studying opportunities, they certainly must know the information. This overconfidence can lead to an early ending to studying, which could then lead to a decrease in success on assessments.[1]

DOI: 10.4324/9781003472056-7

Learning material

SENSES

Sensory memory

ATTENTION
Selection & focus

Working memory

Maintenance rehearsal

Long-term memory

Choke point: Mental effort or concentration is a limited resource.
Solution: Overlearning and practice to make knowledge automatic.

Choke point: Narrow focus of attention limits learning.
Solution: Avoid distractions.

Choke point: Working memory has a limited capacity of about 4 chunks of information.
Solution: Organize information into large chunks (chunking).

Choke point: Forgetting occurs in working memory and long-term memory.
Solution: Distinctive, overlearned memories resist interference.

Pitfall: Multitasking and distractions greatly reduce learning.
Solution: Remove distractions in order to study with full focus.

Pitfall: Students often prefer the least effective study strategies for long-term learning.
Solution: Develop study strategies based on elaborative rehearsal and desirable difficulties.

Pitfall: People are often overconfident when judging their level of understanding (Metacognition).
Solution: Find ways to assess your understanding, use feedback to regulate your learning.

Combating Overconfidence in the Classroom

In my classroom, how do I combat the pitfall of overconfidence? Frequent honest formative assessments to show students what they know and what they don't know. This is an attempt to reveal those holes in their learning that they erroneously believe they don't have. Very simply put, if I ask them a question in any form and they cannot, using only their brain, answer that question, they absolutely should not be confident in their understanding of that topic or concept. For many, this exposure of ignorance is uncomfortable. Maybe it's just human nature, but most people and students don't like to face their deficiencies. We, instead, prefer to focus on our successes.

This definitely also applies to learning. Students prefer easier methods of studying and learning that don't require facing the facts of their lack of knowledge. Think about it, if I'm spending my time rereading and/or highlighting my notes, I'm constantly looking at information that seems familiar to me and I am certainly not confronting my inability to access or retrieve information via questioning. I'm not getting anything wrong. It's comfortable and cognitively easy...not a good recipe for success. As Dr. Richard Feynman once said, "The first principle is that you must not fool yourself and you are the easiest person to fool."[2]

That comfort and ease fools learners into overconfidence, which will only be revealed when they are tasked with using that information without any aids. Many times, in the classroom, this equates to students being surprised on an assessment because they thought they knew the material. Something I find myself saying constantly to my students that addresses this is they'd rather attempt to answer questions now and find out what they know and what they don't know than avoiding the work and finding out on a summative assessment. At that point, it's too late. While that may not sit well with them, through constant work, they usually eventually realize the benefits and become more at ease with this aspect of the process of learning.

Learning material

SENSES

Sensory memory

Choke point: Mental effort or concentration is a limited resource.
Solution: Overlearning and practice to make knowledge automatic.

Choke point: Narrow focus of attention limits learning.
Solution: Avoid distractions.

ATTENTION

Pitfall: Multitasking and distractions greatly reduce learning.
Solution: Remove distractions in order to study with full focus.

Working memory

Choke point: Working memory has a limited capacity of about 4 chunks of information.
Solution: Organize information into large chunks (chunking).

Pitfall: Students often prefer the least effective study strategies for long-term learning.
Solution: Develop study strategies based on elaborative rehearsal and desirable difficulties.

Choke point: Forgetting occurs in working memory and long-term memory.
Solution: Distinctive, overlearned memories resist interference.

Long-term memory

Pitfall: People are often overconfident when judging their level of understanding (Metacognition).
Solution: Find ways to assess your understanding, use feedback to regulate your learning.

CHOKE POINT 4 - FORGETTING OCCURS IN WORKING MEMORY AND LONG-TERM MEMORY

Just because we've worked that information all the way from sensory memory over to long-term memory, that doesn't mean it's necessarily there forever. Unfortunately, forgetting happens. It'd be a lot easier if, once committed to long-term memory, the information was accessible for a seemingly infinite amount of time. But, as pretty much everyone already knows, that is not the case. We forget. And that's ok.

The problem that arises in school, though, is that students and teachers falsely believe that information is known and understood after a single bout of either rereading or recalling of information. And it may be in the short term, but asked hours or days later about that same information will certainly yield a much lower success rate.

Now, I would like to clarify something: I'm not saying we simply accept this and don't work to curtail the forgetting of material. Again, we know it's going to happen, but what can be done to minimize its effects and reintroduce the forgotten information? The biggest bang for your buck in a classroom comes in the form of two strategies that have already been discussed - retrieval practice and spaced practice. These strategies provide an efficient and effective manner for fighting forgetting; with the understanding that we're fighting a never-ending battle in the classroom...and that's okay. It's what we do as teachers and learners. What we can't forget to do is let our students know that it is normal to forget and should be expected. Allowing them in on this little nugget of information can completely change the mindset of the learner (and teacher), providing a more intellectually safe environment for students to assess their learning and more effectively shape their studies.

I want to end Part I with the same quote used to begin it:

> Without knowledge of human cognitive processes, instructional design is blind.

While this may not have made much sense to you if you've never considered memory processing, I hope your newly formed spider web of knowledge about memory has "caught" it and can better relate. I know this may seem obvious now, but memory processing is what it is. There is no magic strategy or activity that works *in spite of* that human cognitive design. Our classroom and instruction must work within these confines. Anything to the contrary is futile, at best. And, since we work in a profession where one of the main goals is to educate people, efficiency and effectiveness of practice should be a top priority. This makes understanding memory processing a must.

In Part II, we dive into how to create an environment that better works within the confines of memory; how the classroom should look, how information should be designed for learners, and more specifically how students should study for remembering and not just for a grade.

Notes

1 Dunlosky, J., & Rawson, K. A. (2012). Overconfidence produces underachievement: Inaccurate self-evaluations undermine students' learning and retention. *Learning and Instruction*, *22*(4), 271-280.

2 Feynman, R. *Cargo cult science* [Speech Transcript]. California Institute of Technology Archives and Special Collections. https://calteches.library. caltech.edu/51/2/CargoCult.htm (Original work published 1974)

Part I Major Points

- Understanding memory processing is vital for efficient and effective instruction and learning.

- Sensing information is a necessary, but insufficient first step in learning.

- Prioritizing attending to the necessary information is paramount for learning.

- Designing a learning environment and instruction with minimal distractions is key to an effective and efficient classroom.

- Humans cannot multitask.

- Working memory is limited in capacity, and avoiding cognitive overload in the learning environment is key.

- Everyone forgets.

- Forgetting still occurs even if the information is ultimately stored in long-term memory.

- Students, generally, do not choose the most effective studying methods and are overconfident in their level of understanding.

DOI: 10.4324/9781003472056-8

PART II
Maximizing Learning

There are so many strategies and activities teachers may use in class once the choke points and pitfalls are accounted for. It can be quite overwhelming to know just what is the best bet for optimizing working memory without overloading it while also making the most of moving the content to long-term memory. Compound that with the fact we are tasked with educating, not one brain, but a classroom full of them. That's a job that only a teacher can understand and appreciate.

For me, early in my teaching career (I am currently in my 19th year of full-time teaching), I certainly didn't know what I didn't know and solely relied on whatever professional development was provided by the school. Even with the best of intentions, for the most part, that development was not what I truly needed to grow as an inexperienced teacher. Most of it focused on what I would call the "bells and whistles" of teaching. "Here are some new methods to make learning fun" and/or "here's how to improve engagement through movement" ...that sort of stuff. And, while there may be a place for some of that sentiment occasionally in the classroom, it certainly does not suffice when students are novice learners, have very weak schemas for the content, and their spider web of knowledge cannot "catch" any information.

What I needed as an inexperienced teacher was more research-based strategies that allowed me to cast a wider net during instruction; to minimize distractions in the classroom so students can attend to what is truly important and then use that information in a way that maximizes the chance it will be stored in long-term memory...not just for some

DOI: 10.4324/9781003472056-9

assessment that is coming up, but also to use as a foundation for adding to and to use in a creative manner, if needed.

As a teacher, having the research of 'what works' is so very comforting. I would hate to believe that what I'm doing in class with my students is potentially ineffective and wasting our time. This reminds me of the quote that started this book: "Without knowledge of human cognitive processes, instructional design is blind."[1] Add to this that, as teachers, we don't know what we don't know, and we are perfectly blissful in our ignorance of how learning happens and what instructional strategies are appropriate or inappropriate at differing points of the learning process.

To be perfectly honest with you, although I have a Master's degree in secondary education, I don't remember having any classes touching on these topics. And, only very infrequently, have I had the pleasure of taking part in any professional development opportunities on the topics of memory processing, cognitive load, learning strategies, et cetera. I have been reliant on finding the research and those knowledgeable on these subjects on my own time, which can be limited. As I said earlier, most of the time, development consists of some new gadget or gismo to use in class or is focused on fun and engagement. And, while I'm not against technology usage in the classroom (when used appropriately, it can certainly add to instruction), I often find that the newest gadget may be applied in opposition to how learning happens or doesn't heighten learning. Usually, the newest gimmick that has been purchased for usage in the classroom is just that...a gimmick for quality and proper instructional practices.

And for teachers looking to do what's best for their students (aren't we all?), the water quickly becomes murky for what to include and what to not include during class. How should we teach this? Should it be fun? Are the students engaged? How do I know? How do they know? It can all be quite overwhelming. I know, for myself, it was when I began to lean on more evidence-based strategies that I gained confidence that what I was doing in the classroom was best for my students.

The murkiness seemed to clear and my confidence grew. It's amazing how, just like a good clinical experiment, the simpler the instruction and practice in the classroom, the better for the whole. It is only when we entangle how we instruct and how students experience content (especially when the information is new) that complications arise and results suffer.

Think about it this way, the more complicated we make it to learn particular content, the more novice students have to keep in their working memory. And, that can quickly become overloaded if they are not only attempting to remember four reasons the Articles of Confederations failed while also trying to remember the rules for this new activity they're doing in class. Chances are, unconsciously, they will have to make decisions about attending to following the instructions or learning the material, not both.

Especially when introducing new material, simple is better. But, don't confuse simple with easy. The two are definitely not the same. It is a simple task to do 50 pushups. Nothing confusing about it. The instructions are clear. The expectations are clear. Fifty pushups. But that does not make it easy. Give it a try. It's difficult. The classroom and instruction should be the same way for new content; streamlined and simple instruction combined with an environment free from choke points and practice with clear expectations while avoiding pitfalls.

Part I talked about what that classroom and study environment should look like and sound like…free from all possible distractions so students can attend to the important material. And Part I also mentioned how students intuitively do not use the most efficient and effective methods for studying and learning. (Students overwhelmingly prefer simple rereading of notes and highlighting.) So, what should students do in class to practice? When should students practice? What should we model for students to see as proper learning either as practice in class or on their own? And how should we talk to our students about all of this? I'm glad you asked. I would love to answer those questions.

Retrieval Practice and Spaced Practice

With over a century of research on this subject, many learning strategies show positive effects in learning.[2] Two strategies seem to rise to the top as the cream of the crop: retrieval practice (sometimes called the testing effect) and spaced practice (sometimes called distributed practice). In an article by cognitive psychologist[3], Dr. John Dunlosky reviewed the efficacy of ten different learning strategies. They can be seen in the following table:

Effectiveness of techniques reviewed

Technique	Extent and conditions of effectiveness
Practice testing	Very effective under a wide array of situations.
Distributed practice	Very effective under a wide array of situations.
Interleaved practice	Promising for Math and concept learning, but needs more research.
Elaborative interrogation	Promising, but needs more research.
Self-explanation	Promising, but needs more research.
Re-reading	Distributed re-reading can be helpful, but time could be better spent using another strategy.
Highlighting and underlining	Not particularly helpful, but can be used as a first step toward further study.
Summarization	Helpful only with training on how to summarize.
Keyword mnemonic	Somewhat helpful for learning languages, but benefits are short-lived.
Imagery for text	Benefits limited to imagery-friendly text, and needs more research.

While all of these strategies may have a time and place in the classroom and with learning, retrieval practice and spaced practice are the only rated as "very effective under a wide array of situations." Because of this, and other similar research, I think it most important to focus on these two strategies in Part II of this book. They are the low hanging fruit that are just ripe for implementation in the classroom to positively impact learning across the board.

Before really breaking down some of the research behind retrieval practice and spaced practice and how I employ these strategies in my classroom, I think it important to understand their value. First of all, as is stated above, these strategies are so widely applicable to students. It doesn't really matter the age or ability level of the student, these strategies improve learning. Here is a compilation of retrieval practice and spaced practice research applied across different ages from pre-k to adult:[4]

Effectiveness of Spacing

Learner level	Learning material	Implementation of Spacing
Preschool or younger (<5 years old)	Pictures	Pictures presented twice, separated by two, four or eight intervening pictures.
	Toy names	Three presentations per toy spaced apart by 30 seconds.
	Words	Four exposures spaced apart by 3 days.
Elementary school (5-10 years old)	Credibility judgements	Three lessons spaced 1 week apart.
	Foreign language translations	Two learning sessions separated by 1 week.
	Grammatical rules	10 practice trials spaced across 5 or 10 days.
	Mathematical skills	Four daily sessions spaced 2-4 hours apart, repeated over 18 days.
	Pictures	Pictures presented twice, separated by two, four or eight intervening pictures.
	Scientific principles	Four lessons spaced across 4 consecutive days.
	Vocabulary words	Two lessons spaced 1 week apart.
Middle school (11-13 years old)	Biology lessons	Four lessons spaced 1 week apart.
	Credibility judgements	Three lessons spaced 1 week apart.
	Foreign language translations	Two sessions spaced apart by 1 day.
	Mathematics, algebra and geometry	Problems per topic spaced across eight assignments over 15 weeks.
	Mathematics, permutations and diagrams	Three practice sessions spaced 1 week apart.
High school (14-18 years old)	Foreign language translations	Three practice periods spaced across 3 consecutive days.
	Mathematics, geometry	Problems per topic spaced across seven assignments over 6 weeks.
	Physics problems	Each practice problem spaced apart by 1 day.
	Writing in shorthand	Multiple exercises spaced apart by up to five consecutive lessons.

Learner level	Learning material	Implementation of Spacing
Under-graduate	Anatomy course	Three learning sessions spaced across 1 week.
	Artists' painting styles	Six examples per artist, presented with intervening examples.
	Educational texts	Two readings separated by 1 week.
	Engineering problems	Three homework sets spaced apart across 3 weeks.
	Face-name pairs	Four presentations per pair, spaced apart by one, three or five intervening items.
	Foreign language verb conjugation	Two sessions spaced apart by 1 week.
	Grammatical rules	Three sessions spaced apart by 1 or 4 weeks.
	Mathematics, pre-calculus	Three quizzes spaced apart by 1-2 weeks.
	Mathematics, permutations	Two practice sessions spaced apart by 1 week.
	Meteorology lessons	Two sessions spaced apart by 8 days.
	Natural categories	Six examples per category, presented with intervening examples.
	Physics problems	Three problems per topic, spaced apart by 2 days or more.
	Piano melodies	Three practice sessions, separated by 6 or 24 hours.
	Pictures	Pictures presented twice, separated by two, four or eight intervening pictures.
	Statistics	Three practice sessions, spaced apart by 2 or 5 days.
	Visuospatial memory task	Four practice trials spaced apart by 15 minutes each.
	Word pairs	Four practice sessions spaced across 4 consecutive days.
	Word-processing skills	Two practice sessions spaced apart by 10 minutes.
Post-graduate	Cardiopulmonary resuscitation skills	Multiple practice sessions, each spaced apart by up to 1 month.
	Nutrition knowledge	Four learning sessions, each spaced apart by 1 week.
	Pharmaceutical names	Two sessions of retrieval practice, separated by 2, 3, 4, 7 or 8 weeks.

Learner level	Learning material	Implementation of Spacing
Post-graduate	Surgical procedures	Four training sessions, each spaced apart by 1 week.
	Urology course	Eleven to thirteen learning exercises, each spaced 1 week post-lesson.
Older adults (>50 years old)	Artists' painting styles	Six examples per artist, presented with intervening examples.
	Motor skill task	Nine practice trials spaced apart by 43 seconds each.
	Visuospatial memory task	Four practice trials spaced apart by 15 minutes each.
	Word pairs	Word pairs presented twice, separated by 1, 4, 8 or 20 intervening pairs.

Effectiveness of Retrieval Practice

Learner level	Learning material	Implementation of Retrieval Practice
Preschool or younger (<5 years old)	Picture names	Cued recall test followed by restudy or immediate answer feedback.
	Toy names	Verbal cued recall test.
	Video demonstrations	Re-enactment of demonstrated behaviours.
Elementary school (5-10 years old)	Educational texts	Fill-in-the-blank test.
	Map features	Map-based cued recall test with feedback.
	Picture names	Verbal free recall test followed by restudy.
	Spelling words	Cued recall test with feedback.
	Symbols	Cued recall test with feedback.
	Word lists	Word stem-completion test.
Middle school (11-13 years old)	Botanical features	Cued recall test involving filling in a diagram.
	Definition-word pairs	Cued recall test with feedback.
	Educational texts	Free recall test.
	Foreign language translations	Cued recall test with feedback.

Learner level	Learning material	Implementation of Retrieval Practice
Middle school (11-13 years old)	Botanical features	Cued recall test involving filling in a diagram.
	Definition-word pairs	Cued recall test with feedback.
	Educational texts	Free recall test.
	Foreign language translations	Cued recall test with feedback.
	History facts	Cued recall test with feedback.
	Science course materials	Multiple-choice clicker test with feedback.
High school (14-18 years old)	Educational texts	Multiple-choice and short answer test.
	History course materials	Multiple-choice and short answer clicker test with feedback.
	Mathematical facts, procedures	Short answer tests followed by restudy.
	Science and history facts	Multiple-choice test.
	Science concepts	Multiple-choice and true-false tests.
	Word lists	Recognition test during verbal shadowing task.
Under-graduate	Anatomy terms	Short-answer test with or without feedback.
	Biology course	Multiple-choice clicker quizzes with feedback.
	Biology facts	Short-answer test with feedback.
	Biology processess	Short-answer test with feedback.
	Chemical engineering problems	Scenario-based problem solving practice test.
	Deductive inferences	Fill-in-the-blank or free recall test with feedback.
	Educational texts	Short-answer test with feedback.
	Face-name pairs	Cued recall test.
	Foreign language translations	Oral cued recall with feedback.
	History facts	Short-answer or multiple-choice test with feedback.
	Map features	Map-based covert cued recall test with feedback.
	Map locations	Virtual judgement of relative direction test with or without feedback.

Learner level	Learning material	Implementation of Retrieval Practice
Under-graduate	Mathematical functions	Function estimation test with feedback.
	Natural categories	Verbal cued recall test with or without feedback.
	Neuroscience course	Multiple-choice or short answer test with feedback.
	Psychology course	Multiple-choice or short answer test with feedback.
	Scientific method	Free recall test followed by restudy.
	Spelling words	Cued recall test with feedback.
	Symbols	Cued recall test.
	Word lists	Free recall test.
	Word pairs	Cued recall test with feedback.
	Word triplets	Cued recall test with feedback.
	Video lectures	Multiple-choice or short answer test with or without feedback.

As you can tell, there has been a plethora of research conducted on these two learning strategies across all age ranges. In addition to the benefits not being limited to certain age ranges, they also improve learning across all ability levels, with some evidence that it actually more greatly improves learning for lower ability students.[5] And the positive impact of these strategies is not limited to memorization of material. There are many studies displaying the positive effects of retrieval and spaced practice improving learning in differing contexts and with near and far transfer of information.[6]

Ease of Application in the Classroom

While a wealth of evidence displaying the positive effects of retrieval practice and spaced practice are important, they don't mean anything to a teacher if they cannot be adequately applied during instruction. I know I have experienced professional development many times where the information and gadget may be really neat, but the practicality of implementation does not apply to my students or simply isn't feasible for some reason.

That is not so with retrieval practice and spaced practice. It does not matter what subject you teach. The gadgets you may or may not have at your disposal does not matter. In fact, it could definitely be argued these strategies are more easily applied without the use of technology at all. There is something lovely about the simplicity of a few pieces of paper and a pen/pencil on a clean desk just waiting to display the work of learning.

A last major reason to utilize these strategies for all is they model for students what proper studying should look like. Chances are students have not been instructed on what is more efficient and effective for learning and they do not know how to study. Seems unlikely, but most students when studying use methods that are a path of least resistance (and, consequentially, utilize lower levels of cognition). There is certainly an honest conversation to be had with students on the "how to" and "when to" of studying. Without that honest conversation and instruction, students will see little reward for their efforts. This, in turn, usually leads to lower levels of motivation for studying and learning...but more on this later.

So, let's really unpack these two strategies. What are they? How are they applied in the classroom setting? When should they be applied? How should students use them when studying at home or at the library? All of these questions, and many more, will be answered.

Notes

1 Sweller, J., Ayres, P., & Kalyuga, S. (2011). *Cognitive load theory*. Springer.

2 Abbott, E. E. (1909). On the analysis of the factor of recall in the learning process. *The Psychological Review: Monograph Supplements, 11*(1), 159-177.

3 Dunlosky, J. (2013). Strengthening the student toolbox: Study strategies to boost learning. *American Educator, 37*(3), 12-21.

4 Carpenter, S. K., Pan, S. C., & Butler, A. C. (2022). The science of effective learning with spacing and retrieval practice. *Nature Reviews Psychology, 1*(9), 496-511.

5 Agarwal, P. K., Finley, J. R., Rose, N. S., & Roediger III, H. L. (2017). Benefits from retrieval practice are greater for students with lower working memory capacity. *Memory, 25*(6), 764-771.

6 Pan, S. C., Agarwal, P. K., & RetrievalPractice.org. (2020). *Retrieval practice and transfer of learning: Fostering students' application of knowledge*. Faculty Works. https://remix.berklee.edu/faculty-works/17

7 Introduction to Retrieval Practice

Simply put, retrieval practice is getting information out of the brain in some form or fashion...cognitively retrieving the material from memory. We tend to think of the learning that occurs in class as only occurring during classroom instruction or when the teacher is teaching, but that is just not so. The act of retrieving the information for usage creates a very powerful situation for learning and more durable processing of material.

Certainly the "getting the information in" portion of a lesson is incredibly important, but do not neglect the significance of the "getting the information out" bit of class for learning. That may be a bit of a shift in your thinking and might change how you structure your class. If that's the case...good. As you'll see time and time again in this book, retrieving the content for usage is essential for an efficient and effective learning environment, whether that be in a school or studying somewhere else.

Assessment Is Not a Bad Word

Now, don't be frightened by what I'm about to tell you. Almost exclusively, when we ask students to get information out of their memory, we are assessing. I know, assessment is sometimes seen as a bad word in education, especially when attributed to an oversaturation of state and national testing. I get that, I really do. But, assessment simply isn't just nationally normed assessments of learning. In fact, assessment should be seen and experienced daily in the effective classroom. Said another

DOI: 10.4324/9781003472056-10

way, we should be asking our students to assess their learning by tasking them with using the content they've gained through class instruction regularly. See, assessment isn't scary, it's essential.

Assessment is an integral part of learning. If we're not assessing student learning, both teachers and students are blind, once again, about the instruction that has been given and what may be provided in the future. Assessment may look like a quick five-question quiz when they enter the room. It may be an informal discussion with a peer about a particular topic of a lesson. It might look like the ability to draw and label a motor neuron or might be students using their gained knowledge to solve a novel problem. Assessment is so malleable in the classroom. And all of this assessment, whether more formal or informal, whether for a grade or not, is a form of retrieval practice. In every setting where assessment is used, students are tasked, in some way, with retrieving and using classroom content.

Now, you may be thinking to yourself, *is he really writing a book telling me to ask my students questions? I already do that.* And, to answer your question simply and somewhat incompletely...yes. That's what I'm saying. But, before you close this book and put it on the shelf to gain dust, hear this: not all retrieval practice is the same.

Depending on what you're hoping to ultimately get out of your students, how you structure their practice, what questions you ask, when you set the task, all matter. So, I hope you are somewhat buoyed with an understanding that what follows isn't some major paradigm shift in how you should be teaching. I'm certainly not saying that you've been doing it all wrong...quite the contrary, actually. It is really just to provide you with more evidence and research to use what you're already probably doing better...more efficiently and effectively, to become more surgical in your classroom.

If you think about it, Part I focused more on being more precise with respect to using what we know about memory processing and cognitive load when designing instruction. That is the "information in" portion of learning. What we're talking about in Part II is the "information out" aspect. And focusing on how to most appropriately apply retrieval practice is like sharpening the instructional scalpel for a specific learning surgery.

Retrieval Practice in the Classroom

So, what does this retrieval practice look like in my classroom? My students are preparing for an AP exam, so I feel it necessary to tailor a lot of my retrieval practice opportunities to the style of questions they will be answering on that exam. The AP Psychology exam requires students to answer a large number of multiple-choice questions. Now, that's not to say that all of the retrieval practice opportunities I provide for my students are in this style. Some are simple recognition of material (multiple-choice, matching, et cetera), while in other instances I task my students with viewing more recall questions (fill in the blank without a word bank, short answer, essay, et cetera). Whether they are able to recognize the correct answer among distractors or recall the answer with no assistance, retrieval of material is occurring.

In most cases, though, recognition is easier than recall. I mean, if I asked my students whether they would like to take a test that is all multiple choice and/or matching versus a test that is all essay, an overwhelming percentage of students would certainly choose the recognition questions as they are easier to decipher correctly. So, should we completely rely on recall questions since they are typically more difficult to answer? Maybe not. Especially when students are retrieving information for the first time on an assessment, blind recall of information can be quite difficult.

Obviously, it is difficult to write an essay about a topic that you know absolutely nothing about. If a student cannot recall the information for usage, then the retrieval opportunity is wasted...because nothing is retrieved. By providing opportunities for recognition of material, students are provided with cues to retrieve information. Cues can be monumental for the retrieval of material. They basically provide a hint at the correct answer or even a chance for comparing and contrasting incorrect and correct information to decipher between. And, as a teacher, I would much rather my students be provided recognition questions to begin with so they can critically think about the content before choosing an answer than be given an essay prompt and have no chance at using the material.

Diminishing Cues Retrieval Practice

One really interesting study I've read that made successful use of the recognition to recall style questions focused on what is called *diminishing cues retrieval practice*.[1] What exactly is diminishing cues retrieval practice and how is it different from other forms of retrieval practice? Well, with standard retrieval practice, usually a student is asked a question and they attempt to retrieve that information from their brain and answer correctly. Very simple; ask question, give answer. Often times, there are no cues provided to assist subjects with retrieval. Basically, this standard retrieval practice provides recall attempts. With diminishing cues retrieval practice, though, subjects are provided varying amounts of cues or hints to assist with retrieval practice before final assessment of learning. Usually, this form of retrieval practice begins with more cues, and as more retrieval is attempted of a particular concept or topic, the cues diminish.

Researchers tested the effects of diminishing cues retrieval practice versus accumulating cues retrieval practice and a restudy group. Participants were tasked with associating English words with their Inupiaq counterpart (e.g., dust = apyuq). With diminishing cues retrieval practice, subjects were to first practice with "dust = apyuq" and then later with "dust = apyu_" and then "dust = apy_ _." This pattern was followed during practice trials until there were no cues (dust = _ _ _ _ _).

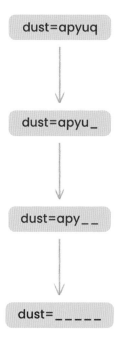

Accumulating cues retrieval practice worked in an exactly opposite manner. Participants began with no cues and practiced until they were provided all cues for retrieval. Finally, in the restudy group, participants were given both the English word and their Inupiaq counterpart continually.

The results? Both diminishing cues and accumulating cues retrieval practice showed better recall than the restudy group...which is not too surprising and is supported by most studies comparing any type of retrieval practice with restudy groups on recall. What was interesting was diminishing cues recall was better than accumulating cues recall when no feedback was given. In addition, during a second experiment where corrective feedback was provided, diminishing cues retrieval practice again outperformed accumulating cues recall and study-only recall. So, in this study across two experiments, diminishing cues during retrieval practice appears to support greater long-term retention of material than accumulating cues retrieval practice and simple restudy of material.

But does diminishing cues retrieval practice outperform standard retrieval practice?

The above study did not test for this condition, but another study did.[2]

This study created three different learning scenarios, with each study corresponding to a greater likelihood of experiencing a testing effect. In experiment 1, researchers did not expect to see the testing effect since initial retrievability was less than 50% and feedback was not provided. In experiment 2, researchers believed the testing effect was more likely to be observed because initial retrievability was greater than 50%, but feedback was still not provided. Finally, in experiment 3, researchers believed a testing effect was quite probable. Initial retrievability was less than 50%, but participants were provided item-by-item feedback. Similar to the first study, the present study tested the recall of differing word pair. The three different practice methods were restudy – standard retrieval practice – diminishing cues retrieval practice.

Their findings? Diminishing cues retrieval practice outperformed both standard retrieval practice and restudy conditions in experiments 1 and 2. It was also more effective than restudy and just as effective as standard retrieval practice in experiment 3. Researchers hypothesized that the success of diminishing cues retrieval practice over standard retrieval practice may be due to the belief that diminishing cues retrieval practice mitigates the possibility of low initial retrievability since, upon first practice, participants are given many cues to increase retrieval success.

In experiment 1, initial retrievability was 25% across participants, yet subjects remembered 44% more information when they studied using diminishing cues retrieval practice instead of standard retrieval practice. With diminishing cues retrieval practice, learners experience a scaffolding of cues which appear to support long-term retention of material more effectively than standard retrieval practice. Learners are provided many cues that support initial retrievability, but over the course or practice, retrieval demands increase as cues decrease.

These studies provide evidence that diminishing cues retrieval practice provides "a more generally effective means of implementing retrieval practice – one that works across a wider range of the task difficulty spectrum...When a task is sufficiently difficult such that retrieval of items during practice is unlikely, learners benefit from the accumulation of retrieval demands (diminishing cues) that grow over the course of practice."[3]

Let me provide a disclaimer at this point: once you start really diving into the evidence surrounding...really, anything in education, it can get a little (or a lot) confusing. Did I just provide you with evidence from a couple of studies that diminishing cues retrieval practice is superior to other types of retrieval practice in certain instances? Yes, I did. Does that mean you can or should always use this form of retrieval practice? Certainly not. As you well know, many variables can hinder the ability to set up diminishing cues retrieval practice opportunities for your students. Probably the most pressing is time. It takes time to set up all of these tasks for students. Sometimes, in the interest of instruction and time and your particular students, standard retrieval practice may fit the bill.

That. Is. Fine.

I guess what I'm saying is, don't get caught up in the minutia of it all. Over a century of research indicates that retrieval practice, in any form, is almost always superior to simple restudy of information and it is always better than doing nothing.

Brain – Book – Buddy

Before I go into some specific examples of what this looks like in my classroom, I want to introduce a strategy that I include with all retrieval practice opportunities. I call it Brain – Book – Buddy. It does not have anything to do with the types of questions you ask, but is more aligned with how students think when retrieving. And, to be honest, Brain – Book – Buddy might be the most important strategy I teach my students. It is so widely applicable across all age ranges (with a little modification) and content areas. It provides a template for proper study habits not only in my class, but for the rest of their lives. And, it elicits an honest assessment of their learning.

So, what exactly is Brain – Book – Buddy?

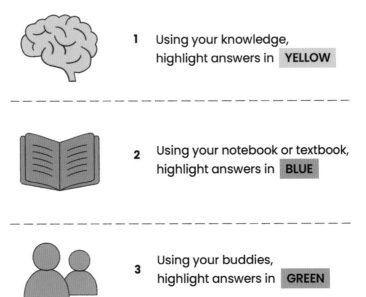

1 Using your knowledge, highlight answers in YELLOW

2 Using your notebook or textbook, highlight answers in BLUE

3 Using your buddies, highlight answers in GREEN

Brain

Brain – Book – Buddy tasks students with completing any assessment on paper three times. The first time using only their brain...or only what they know. I instruct my students to pretend (although this strategy is always used with low-stakes formative assessment) this is the summative assessment; let's see what you know right now. If this was the chapter test or for a grade in the gradebook, how would you do? Whatever they can answer correctly at this point is what they can feel confident they know, with one caveat...guessing...more on how I combat guessing later.

When they finish going through the assessment the first time, using only their brain, I usually have them highlight those answers in a particular color. In the image above, that color is yellow. By highlighting these answers now, when they go through the rest of the tasks of Brain – Book – Buddy, they don't fool themselves into thinking they knew something they didn't know using only their brain.

How often do students complete an assignment using notes or working in a collaborative group and when they finish, they see they have all of the correct answers and they believe they know all of the material because they've earned a 100. Well, not exactly, not if they had to look up three of the answers on the internet and had to ask their peers for two other answers. They didn't really know it all, but they believe they did.

Book

The second time through the assessment, students can use their note-book/notes to both look up any answers they didn't know when using only their brain, and to check their answers from the first time through. This lets the students know what their notes knew, but they didn't know. Again, I'll have students highlight these answers in a different color. Above, the color is blue. At this point, I usually ask students to analyze this data. Why did your notebook have the answer to number seven, but you didn't know the answer on your own? What does this tell you about the notes you write down in class? Is simply writing it down a substitute for study? Probably not. What if they didn't have the answer in their notes? Why did your peers have it written down in their notes, but you did not? Did you lose focus in class? What does this tell you about your learning and what you need to do to be more successful? All of these questions are worthy of a conversation with your students...and they're not having this conversation with themselves naturally. They need to explicitly be asked these questions and provided time to really assess their learning.

Buddy

Lastly, students can turn to their "buddy" to ask for an explanation and answers to any questions that neither their brain nor notebook knew. These answers are highlighted, too. In the image above, that color is green. Like before, there are questions I want to explicitly ask my students and habits I want them to form when considering what they know and what they don't know, what they can answer and what they cannot answer. Why did you not know the answer using your brain and note-book? Were you absent when we covered this material? If you were absent, what does this tell you about your responsibilities when you returned to school? I want students not only thinking about what they can and cannot answer correctly, but what this analysis tells them about their learning.

Usually, by the third time through Brain – Book – Buddy, all students have all of the answers written down correctly. But, just to make it very obvious to the students what they actually knew, I have them write down three different grades at the top of their paper; one for the use of their brain, one for their notebook, and one for the use of their buddy's knowledge. I'll usually finish up with a statement like, "You ended this assessment with all of the questions answered correctly and that is certainly important for learning, but don't be fooled. You only really knew what you answered using only your brain. That would be your true grade, if we were to post in the gradebook."

And, finally, "Now what are you going to do with the material you couldn't answer correctly? How does that impact your future studies?" Hopefully, that material goes to the top of their to-be studied pile and the questions they answered correctly can become secondary material to study...but it does need to be looked at again because we are all humans and humans forget.

Did You Guess?

On its own, I believe adding Brain – Book – Buddy to any and all relevant assessment opportunities is worth it. One addition I make to this and other formative assessments in class is simply to pose this question to my students: *Did you guess?*

A simple question with possibly large ramifications for the reliability of a student's effort. Again, we want assessments that show a real and true level of knowledge. Guessing an answer correctly doesn't indicate a confident amount of understanding about a topic. Usually, depending on the type of formative assessment, I'll simply ask students (before we cover the answers) to maybe place an asterisk beside all questions that they are less than 75% sure of the answer. The percentage isn't really all that important. I've just found it to be easier for students to understand "what's a guess?" when it is quantified in some manner. That way, once we've had a discussion on the correct answers to the assessment, students again aren't fooled into believing they confidently knew more than they actually knew. They might have earned a 90 on the assessment, but if they look back at where they placed asterisks, they may see that three of the answers they got correct were based on a guess.

Again, while it's good they got those questions correct, they should not fool themselves into believing they really knew the material. They just got lucky and luck isn't representative of an honest assessment of their knowledge.

An Honest Assessment

Both Brain – Book – Buddy and Did You Guess? are an attempt to have honest conversations and honest assessments with my students about what effective learning and studying really look like. Of course, there is some hesitation by the students at first. It isn't very fun to find out what you don't know. It is much easier, both cognitively and emotionally, to simply reread notes or the textbook, but that certainly doesn't offer a clear and reliable assessment of knowledge. And it also doesn't serve as effective an event for learning.

So, while students find themselves wanting to avoid simple, but effective, retrieval practice, I explicitly state that they'd rather be honest with themselves during low stakes formative assessment to truly know what they know and what they don't know than avoid this to only find out on the summative assessment they don't understand some bits of content. If they only find out on the summative assessment they don't know some of the material, it's probably too late. And so it is with most things we do. The ballerina doesn't wait until the recital to begin practicing the routine. They don't just watch a video of the performance and say, "Ok, I got it." They practice over and over again until they prove to themselves (and their teacher) they can do it. Learning classroom content shouldn't be any different. More cognitively effortful practice produces better results than less arduous attempts at learning.

For both the benefit of the students and teacher, the highly effective and efficient classroom is absent of assumption of learning. *Assuming is the enemy of learning.* When students only use their brain to answer questions and/or identify when they are guessing, there's no assuming. They can either answer the questions or participate in the discussion or apply the content or they cannot. When retrieval practice and assessment is done correctly, assuming is minimal and honesty is maximized.

Unknown Unknowns to Known Knowns

Seen more explicitly, retrieval practice helps students see their *known knowns, their known unknowns,* and *their unknown unknowns.* This is something I will also focus on with my students. It helps them to see this process of assessment for learning in several different ways. I first read about this in *Make It Stick.*[4] There was a wonderful quote by Donald Rumsfeld that, while not talking about teaching and learning, certainly applies:

> There are known knowns; there are things we know that we know. There are known unknowns; that is to say, there are things that we now know we don't know. But there are also unknown unknowns – there are things we do not know we don't know.

How does this idea apply to students and learning? I like to present the idea to my students this way:

Known Knowns

What do you now know that you know? The known knowns are those questions they knew and answered correctly. A lot of times this is of no surprise to the students, but sometimes they know information they didn't realize they understood. An important caveat is to ensure students don't consider questions they guessed and answered correctly as known knowns. If a student has to guess to get it correct, they don't really know it.

Known Unknowns

What do you now know that you don't know? This is where the assessment of their knowledge goes to the next level. Again, it is much more pleasant to look at the material answered correctly on an assessment (known knowns). But this does not utilize perhaps the most important aspect of assessment...the known unknowns. By having a look at the questions they answered incorrectly, students have now identified what they know they don't know. Now, they know better what to study. They can focus their time and efforts on the known unknowns instead of using their valuable time on the known knowns. It sounds easy to complete this exercise after an assessment, but it is not intuitive. This is something that needs to be explicitly spoken about and practiced in class to become second nature to students.

Unknown Unknowns

This is a more difficult category to identify. I see the unknown unknown information as vast holes in the student's learning. Perhaps they missed a lesson or two of material or maybe the formative assessment involved an essay where the student completely omitted a chunk of information. In my best estimation, a student's unknown unknowns can only be found by someone or something outside of themselves; usually brought up by the teacher or perhaps by peers during discussions. I think this may best be illustrated in the classroom by a student having that ah-ha moment of, "Oh, I didn't even realize that was something we needed to know."

Ultimately, a major goal of breaking down formative assessment in this manner should be to (1) identify unknown unknowns, (2) practice known unknowns, and (3) apply known knowns in differing context to elicit transfer of learning.

Assessment should:

Identify		Practice		Apply
unknown unknowns	⟶	known unknowns	⟶	known knowns

Unknown unknowns	Known unknowns	Known knowns
Material students didn't know they needed to know and answered incorrectly.	Material students thought they knew but answered incorrectly.	Material students answered correctly.
Identifying this information is an important step in the learning process.	Practicing this information is paramount for retention.	Applying this information in differing scenarios and settings can lead to deeper processing.
Students should question why they didn't know they needed to know this and include this material when studying in the future.	Students should question why they didn't remember this and tailor their studies to include multiple effortful recall and/or recognition opportunities of this material.	Students should continue to use this subject matter to ensure understanding and strengthen retention of material.

After completing an informal assessment, I will sometimes have my students draw a chart with three columns; one for unknown unknowns, one for known unknowns, and one for known knowns. Students are tasked with placing different topics/concepts, people, terms, ideas, et cetera from the retrieval practice opportunity into these three categories.

I've found it important that students don't just write down the numbers of the questions in the different columns, but they should write down the specific content (names, key terms, et cetera) of the questions. This makes it much easier for students to use this chart when coming back to this information later for studying. Of course, students should first look at the unknown unknowns and the known unknowns when studying before again looking at the known knowns. This provides an honest assessment of their knowledge. Assumption of learning is low with this self-assessment and students again are provided an opportunity to create proper habits for what learning is and what it is not; what studying is and what it is not.

Retrieval Practice Is Communication

At its heart, *retrieval practice is communication* and Brain – Book – Buddy, Did You Guess?, and Known Knowns to Unknown Unknowns are prime strategies to use with students, no matter their age or ability level. These strategies communicate to the teacher what the students know and don't know. It communicates to the students what they know and don't know. This is key to the efficient and effective classroom and to the student studying who wants to make the most of their time. It is important that, during class, we take these measures of knowledge quite frequently. When you think about it, not assessing (and listening to what that is communicating) is akin to driving to an unknown destination without any form of map; you don't know where you're going and you don't know when you'll get there. If we don't assess frequently in class, both students and teacher are unaware of what students should know and they don't know how much of that they actually know.

Notes

1 Finley, J. R., Benjamin, A. S., Hays, M. J., Bjork, R. A., & Kornell, N. (2011). Benefits of accumulating versus diminishing cues in recall. *Journal of Memory and Language, 64*(4), 289–298.

2 Fiechter, J. L., & Benjamin, A. S. (2018). Diminishing-cues retrieval practice: A memory-enhancing technique that works when regular testing doesn't. *Psychonomic Bulletin & Review, 25*, 1868–1876.

3 Fiechter, J. L., & Benjamin, A. S. (2018). Diminishing-cues retrieval practice: A memory-enhancing technique that works when regular testing doesn't. *Psychonomic Bulletin & Review, 25*, 1868–1876.

4 Brown, P. C., Roediger III, H. L., & McDaniel, M. A. (2014). *Make it stick: The science of successful learning*. The Belknap Press of Harvard University Press.

8 Anxiety, Stress-Resistant Memories, and Collaboration

Before I get into specific activities I use to task my students with retrieval practice opportunities, I want to include one more reason to utilize retrieval practice in the classroom: there is evidence indicating it decreases test anxiety and stress. Now, I know this may seem contrary to what we often hear about questioning and assessment, but let's look at the research before passing judgement.

Test anxiety is quite common. Students become apprehensive about a quiz, a big chapter test, the SAT, AP exams, the ACT, et cetera. Or if you're in the UK, perhaps students are worried in preparing for their GCSEs or A Levels. This nervousness can negatively impact student performance on those tests and can even negatively skew their feelings about school and education in general. Although there are those who question whether we should stop testing altogether, it's not happening anytime soon.

So, what can help with this test anxiety? Retrieval practice. In an article published in 2014, retrieval practice had quite the positive effect on test anxiety experienced by teenage students.[1] Data collected from 1408 students between the ages of 11–18 showed 72% of students reported retrieval practice made them less nervous for tests and exams, 22% of students indicated they experienced about the same amount of test anxiety, and 6% said retrieval practice made them more nervous. The pattern was consistent across content areas, gender, and students receiving special services. In addition to these numbers, 81% of students reported they felt the same amount of test anxiety or less in

DOI: 10.4324/9781003472056-11

the class that used retrieval practice relative to their other classes. The findings from this study indicate that, contrary to the somewhat popular notion that assessment seems to increase student anxiety, the opposite is quite true in classrooms where retrieval practice is commonly utilized.

How do students feel about Retrieval Practice?

After using Retrieval Practice, do students feel less anxious, the same, or more anxious?

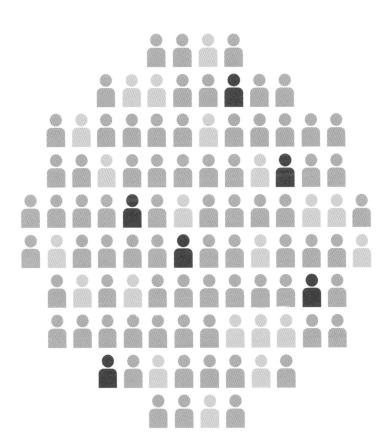

Stress-Resistant Memories

Another study, from 2016, takes a look at retrieval practices' possible ability to produce "stress-resistant memories."[2] Much research has shown that stress can negatively impact memory retrieval. This study wondered if how the material was encoded affected the memory's ability to be retrieved. So, they chose retrieval practice because "it had the most potential to create memories that were resilient to stress." One hundred twenty participants studied either 30 concrete nouns or 30 images of nouns. Sixty of the participants studied via restudy methods...basically just looking over the items. The other 60 participants studied with retrieval practice...attempts to recall as many items as possible.

This procedure was repeated to study the other (either concrete nouns or images of nouns) items that had not been already studied. After a short distractor task, participants were allowed to restudy all 60 items in their method of study. After 24 hours, 30 restudy and 30 retrieval practice participants underwent stress induction while the other 30 restudy and 30 retrieval practice participants completed a time-matched non-stressful task. So, the experiment had four groups – 30 restudy with stress, 30 restudy without stress, 30 retrieval practice with stress, and 30 retrieval practice without stress. Five minutes into the stress induction or control task, all participants completed test one, in which they attempted to identify words or images they studied 24 hours prior. Twenty minutes later, participants repeated the process for test one, but for the words or images they did not see in test one. This is indicated as test two.

The results?

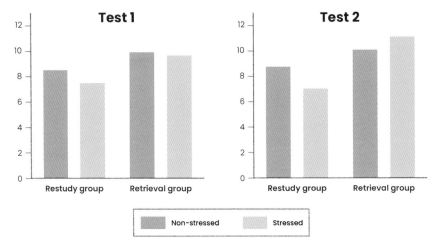

The study points out three key findings:

1) On test two, stressed restudy participants recalled fewer items than non-stressed restudy participants (7.0–8.7). This difference was not as evident on test two in the retrieval group (10.3–11.1). Notice also the stressed retrieval practice group outperformed the non-stressed restudy group (10.3–8.7).

2) There was little to no difference in memory performance for stressed versus non-stressed participants in test one. Stress neither impaired nor enhanced memory five minutes after stress induction.

3) This study replicates the testing effect. Participants who encoded through retrieval practice recalled significantly more words and images than those who encoded through restudy techniques.

The data from this study also appears counter to what intuition may tell us about stress and retrieval of information. "We did not find this effect when stress acted on strong memory representations or when memory was assessed immediately after the onset of stress. Regarding the former, we showed that using a highly effective learning strategy to

strengthen memory at encoding inoculated memory against the delete-
rious effects of the delayed stress response."[3] So, using retrieval practice doesn't impair our ability to recall information, it actually does the
opposite.

But why/how does retrieval practice "inoculate" memory retrieval
against stress? "When attempting to recall an item from memory,
evidence suggests that associated and/or contextual information accompanies that attempt. More retrieval attempts thus create more distinct routes by which the same item can be accessed.
Supporting this, a neuroimaging study found that, relative to
study practice, retrieval practice increased hippocampal connec-
tivity with other brain regions. In the case of our study, retrieval
practice may have created multiple, contextually distinct retrieval
pathways by which to access information. Although cortisol
may have disrupted access to information by certain pathways,
the robustness of the memory representation created by retrieval
practice may have facilitated access to that information by alternate,
undisrupted routes."[4] Wow. Just wow. So, retrieval practice appears
to create more distinct routes to the information to be retrieved. Even
if cortisol impairs one or more pathways, another may still be viable
for retrieval. As a person who focuses mostly on the cognitive psychology side of things, this dip into neuroscience is just fascinating.

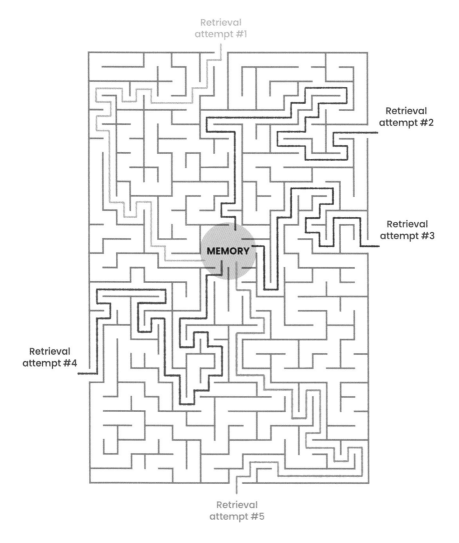

I must add some caution here, though. While researchers are finding out so much more about our brain and how it impacts our emotions and cognition, the general consensus is that we are still in the early days of really seeing the big picture of how findings from the neuroscience community might directly impact learning. So, with everything you see/read, use caution. This work is certainly fascinating and, in the future, I believe we will know so much more in this arena...we're just not all the way there, yet.

Retrieval Practice in the Collaborative Setting

While much of the research and activities I will provide later will focus on retrieval practice as an individual endeavor, it certainly also has its place in the collaborative setting. A 2017 study looked specifically at this aspect of retrieval practice.[5] Researchers conducted three experiments to test how students in collaborative groups were impacted by either retrieving information to answer aloud (overt retrieval) or as a listener/monitor of a speaker's response (covert retrieval). How would recall be affected when assessed either after three minutes or two days?

In experiments one and two, subjects asked to overtly retrieve information (state their answer out loud) accurately recalled more than subjects tasked with covert retrieval (simply listening for accuracy or fluidity of information from the subject overtly retrieving) when assessed after a two-day retention interval. In other words, if you've got two students quizzing each other, the student asking the questions and listening for the answer is not retaining as much information as the student tasked with recalling and answering the question aloud.

When I think about it, these results make sense to me. The person simply reading the questions and hearing a response is not actively retrieving a memory, so there is no memory to strengthen. Only the participant tasked with overtly accessing and stating the answer to the questions has to perform the retrieval, and that student reaps the reward of that action.

In experiment three, the researchers changed the task of the listener. Instead of simply assessing the answer of the subject overtly retrieving, now the covert retriever was asked to monitor and answer silently themselves. They were also asked to record by circling either "yes" or "no" on a piece of paper whether they were able to recall the answer. Completing this task essentially created a situation where both subjects were asked to come up with an answer, but only one verbalized it. The results? Unlike experiments one and two, where the subject overtly retrieving scored better than the covert retriever, in experiment three, both subjects scored quite similarly. The cognition involved in recalling and retrieving the answer led to the learning, not simply the overt retrieval.

Now, I'm not much for quotes, but one does seem to fit here:

> The person doing the thinking is doing the learning.

You may have read a very similar quote. "The person doing the **talking** is doing the learning." While talking can certainly indicate a level of knowledge for a particular topic, verbalizing material shouldn't necessarily be the standard we're looking for in the classroom. It's really the cognition the students are doing that matter and that they are assessed properly on that knowledge. As the research above indicates, thinking about the information and mentally working with the material is what ultimately leads to long-term retention of material. Whether students demonstrate the act of retrieval through speech or writing down an answer doesn't seem to matter.

Now for the really important question: **how does this apply to the classroom and to collaborative work?**

- When a question is presented to the whole class, give time for all to ponder and write their answer down on paper before asking for one student to verbalize the answer.

- When students are reviewing with partners or in a larger group, give all participants a task that involves thinking about/with the material. This may look like students writing their answer down on paper before revealing it to all.

- Very practically, instead of using flashcards in a manner where one student holds the cards and presents them for another student to answer verbally (think overt and covert retrieval), simply place the cards on the table and have both students write their answer down before flipping over the card.

The common thread in all of these activities is cognition...requiring all to access material from their memory. In my opinion, that should be a main focus of the classroom and guide instruction on a daily basis.

Notes

1 Agarwal, P. K., D'antonio, L., Roediger III, H. L., McDermott, K. B., & McDaniel, M. A. (2014). Classroom-based programs of retrieval practice reduce middle school and high school students' test anxiety. *Journal of Applied Research in Memory and Cognition, 3*(3), 131–139.

2 Smith, A. M., Floerke, V. A., & Thomas, A. K. (2016). Retrieval practice protects memory against acute stress. *Science, 354*(6315), 1046–1048.

3 Smith, A. M., Floerke, V. A., & Thomas, A. K. (2016). Retrieval practice protects memory against acute stress. *Science, 354*(6315), 1047.

4 Smith, A. M., Floerke, V. A., & Thomas, A. K. (2016). Retrieval practice protects memory against acute stress. *Science, 354*(6315), 1047.

5 Abel, M., & Roediger III, H. L. (2018). The testing effect in a social setting: Does retrieval practice benefit a listener? *Journal of Experimental Psychology: Applied, 24*(3), 347.

9 Improving upon Multiple-Choice Questioning

So, I'm obviously a big advocate for retrieval practice, but what does this tangibly look like in my classroom? In this chapter, I'll give some examples of activities I use to provide opportunities for my students to retrieve information and provide an assessment of their knowledge level. Obviously, I've tailored these activities for my students in my school...but I believe them to be easily adaptable for differing ability levels and content areas. Although I teach AP Psychology, this certainly does not only apply to content related to psychology. Please use and manipulate any of this material to best fit your learners, your content, and your classroom environment.

I think it is incredibly important I include multiple-choice questioning as a main form of retrieval practice in my classroom since my students are preparing for a major assessment (the AP Psychology exam) that includes a preponderance of this style of question. And, I'm aware that multiple-choice questions are not always the best/truest measure of knowledge. There is obvious room for guessing and a fair amount of luck. I mean, look at the question below:

Billy diligently practices his guitar playing to avoid the bad feelings associated with poor performance during a concert. In this case, his behavior is being shaped by what type of consequence:

A) Positive reinforcement

DOI: 10.4324/9781003472056-12

B) Negative reinforcement
C) Positive punishment
D) Negative punishment
E) Primary reinforcement

Without having any knowledge of this content, one can guess with, on average, a 20% success rate. That is obviously not ideal for a truly honest assessment of learning. So, while I have my students answer multiple-choice questions frequently, I do employ some specific strategies to get more, cognitively, out of the endeavor.

Recognition to Recall

A first, incredibly simple, modification to the typical multiple-choice question assists with turning what is an exercise in recognition into a challenge to recall information. It really decreases the chances a guess at the answer will yield a successful result. I like doing this with my students as a class at first so they firmly grasp how to utilize this method.

But, as I'm sure you'll see, it can very easily be converted to an individual task. So, here's how this goes:

Instead of showing the question stem with all possible answers, I only provide the stem to begin, so it looks something like this:

> Billy diligently practices his guitar playing to avoid the bad feelings associated with poor performance during a concert. In this case, his behavior is being shaped by what type of consequence?

Give the students 20-30 seconds to consider the question and write down what answer they believe will be correct. Only providing the stem makes this a recall question. If students can, using only their brain, come up with the answer, this really indicates a firm understanding of the material. If they cannot come up with any possible correct answers, that also communicates to students their level of understanding.

Occasionally, some stems may provide an opportunity for multiple answer choices to be correct. If this is the case, I encourage students to write down all possible answers. Doing this makes good use of what's called the goal-free effect. (This will be further explained later in this chapter.) The more correct information students can recall at this point is a positive and speaks to a deeper understanding of the information with an ability to transfer their knowledge to multiple situations. And, while there is research suggesting that providing multiple-choice questions with numerous possible correct answers isn't best, for this exercise, I believe it is necessary because it allows students to do more thinking and cognition with the content.

The next step allows for students to see all the possible answers associated and really makes this a multiple-choice question:

> Billy diligently practices his guitar playing to avoid the bad feelings associated with poor performance during a concert. In this case, his behavior is being shaped by what type of consequence:
>
> A) Positive reinforcement
> B) Negative reinforcement
> C) Positive punishment
> D) Negative punishment
> E) Primary reinforcement

Now, if students could provide an answer when the answer choices were removed, they should be able to see if that answer is provided. This provides further indication that their level of understanding is sufficient. If they couldn't provide an answer when the stem alone was presented, I stress to students to not give up now that they are provided. This is still an assessment that can lead to learning and seeing all the possible answers may provide a retrieval cue that allows them to answer confidently and strengthen that material in their memory; maybe to the point that they do not need the options visible the next opportunity they have to retrieve this information.

That's really it. It's simple and provides students with an opportunity to sort of stretch their knowledge by attempting the recall question before providing the answer options and an attempt at recognizing the answer. Again, I stress with my students that this is not only a measure of what you know and, possibly, how well you know it. The act of retrieving the correct answer and all possible information related to that is an act of learning and greatly strengthens the ability to retrieve that information when needed in the future.

Before leaving this activity, which is usually done as a review of information, I will ask students to consider at what point they could correctly answer the questions. Those they could not answer correctly (even after the options were provided) should be at the top of their to-be studied pile, questions they answered correctly after the options were provided should probably be beneath those, and the questions answered correctly without the options should be the bottom priority for study.

Providing a discussion and opportunity for students to think about what these in class assessments mean for their current understanding and future studies is so important. Again, they aren't unconsciously or intuitively analyzing this data. It's got to be explicit and it's got to be modeled and practiced for it to become their habit.

Interacting with All Answer Choices

Another tweak of the classic multiple-choice question that I've found in class to be especially helpful for breaking down complex and confusing information tasks students with interacting cognitively with all possible answer choices. So, not only do they find the correct answer, but then they need to use all of the incorrect answers in a meaningful manner. Doing so helps them to strengthen their understanding and memory of all of the information and also assists students with seeing this activity as a learning event and not just an assessment geared toward finding one correct answer.

So, here's a template for what this looks like for me. You can see that the question is written at the top and all of the tasks are provided below.

Interacting with all answer choices

1   Write question here...   ?

- A.
- B.
- C.
- D.
- E.

Write correct answer here...   Provide a memory aid used OR an illustration of the answer.

Write incorrect answer here...   Why might someone incorrectly choose this answer?

What is tricky or confusing about this answer that makes it the 'best' wrong answer?

Write incorrect answer here...   Rewrite the question to make this incorrect answer the correct answer.

Write incorrect answer here...   Give an example relating this answer to your life.

Write incorrect answer here...   Link this answer to information from a previous lesson/unit or class.

How does this information relae to prior material?

Students, in their analysis of the possible answers, will choose what they believe to be the best answer and then need to provide some sort of mnemonic or memory aid they used to remember this as the answer and/or draw some illustration of the answer. This adds more context to the spider web of this knowledge and further strengthens the memory of this information. Sort of a "what did you think of to help you retrieve this answer?" opportunity. This can help with strengthening the retrieval cue(s) used to access the answer.

Students have a bit of choice in deciding how they will use the incorrect answers, or distractors. The tasks provide quite an array of undertakings and students will really fester over which distractor to use with each. And, while I don't want them to spend too much time strategizing with which answer choice to use where, I do appreciate students engaging with figuring out which answers best fit with the differing tasks. The first task asks students to find the best wrong answer, or the trickiest answer, and then to explain why they might choose this answer.

I love this because it makes students really analyze and separate what is right from wrong and have a firm understanding of what differentiates aspects of all the answers. The next option really kind of reverses that process by tasking students with taking a wrong answer and rewriting the question to make this option the correct answer. The third task helps students with considering how this information relates to their life. Perhaps they'll provide an example of a time when they've experienced this option in their life. In any case, they are using background knowledge, accessing that spider web of knowledge, and adding new context to their understanding of the material.

The last task requires students to think back to past lessons and material to see if this information maybe led to where we are in content with this review. By connecting the dots from where we were in class to where we are in class, students are forced to see the bigger picture of the content.

This activity takes more of an investment in time to set up and execute. You would not want to set ten questions like this for a class to complete.

If done correctly, each question takes around five to ten minutes to adequately answer. So, I reserve this for only the more confusing content of if there's a topic or concept that is especially complex. This is also a nice one to have students revisit as a review before a summative assessment. It packs a large punch of retrieving a lot of content in just a few questions.

Reverse Engineering the Multiple-Choice Question

A last strategy of modifying the classic multiple-choice question asks students to reverse engineer the process. Instead of one stem provided with multiple answers to choose among, students are shown multiple answers and are tasked with writing multiple questions making each answer correct. It usually looks something like this:

Construct a question or scenario where one of the following responses is correct and the distractors are incorrect, but plausible. Do this for each of the possible answers below. In total, there should be five questions, each with a different correct answer.

A) schizophrenia
B) bipolar disorder
C) generalized anxiety disorder
D) obsessive-compulsive disorder
E) major depressive disorder

I usually also provide a template for the students. This makes the task much easier to organize and complete. It looks something like this:

1 Write question here...   ?

A. Schizophrenia
B. Bipolar disorder
C. Generalized anxiety disorder
D. Obsessive-compulsive disorder
E. Major depressive disorder

2 Write question here...   ?

A. Schizophrenia
B. Bipolar disorder
C. Generalized anxiety disorder
D. Obsessive-compulsive disorder
E. Major depressive disorder

3 Write question here...   ?

A. Schizophrenia
B. Bipolar disorder
C. Generalized anxiety disorder
D. Obsessive-compulsive disorder
E. Major depressive disorder

4 Write question here...   ?

A. Schizophrenia
B. Bipolar disorder
C. Generalized anxiety disorder
D. Obsessive-compulsive disorder
E. Major depressive disorder

5 Write question here...   ?

A. Schizophrenia
B. Bipolar disorder
C. Generalized anxiety disorder
D. Obsessive-compulsive disorder
E. Major depressive disorder

Again, quite simple and fairly easy to assign as a teacher. I see a lot of positives with having students reverse engineer multiple choice questions:

1) It helps them to better understand how they are constructed when they are answering.
2) It ensures students understand the material. It would be quite difficult for me to write a question about specific symptoms of, say, schizophrenia if I don't know symptoms of schizophrenia that do not apply to any of the other disorders listed.
3) In order to correctly complete, students are required to not only understand one of the responses, but all of them to be able to compare and contrast characteristics.

Here's one option for taking this and growing it in class to something really special:

• Students could be given smaller sheets of paper with one set of responses and students construct one stem. Then the classes questions could be gathered and shuffled, and a class discussion could occur looking at the different multiple-choice questions that were created. This is especially interesting to me because there are several ways students could consider the example above. Students may choose to write stems focusing on the symptoms of the disorders, the prevalence of the disorders, the genetic components, the environmental components, or general statistics about the different disorders. Having students consider others' questions could perhaps open their minds to differing points of views or facets of concepts.

Also, in an attempt to deepen some student's engagement with the questions, tell them the better questions created may become assessment questions in class. Students may be motivated to give more effort in question construction and/or any activity where the questions are used.

At the end of the day, however you use the task of reverse engineering the multiple-choice question, students are thinking and applying the knowledge they have in their brain; retrieving a lot of information and using it to demonstrate their level of understanding to themselves and the teacher. A great way to end this activity would definitely be to have students consider what information was particularly tricky for them to either remember or write a stem about. This may indicate a hole in their knowledge that needs to be addressed. While this may not have looked like a traditional assessment of their knowledge, it definitely was. Let them know this and encourage students to use assessments requiring the retrieval of information for studying instead of less effective methods that utilize a lower level of cognition (rereading and highlighting, for example).

10 Brain Dump, Color Coding, and What to Retrieve?

A common thread running through all of the strategies mentioned in the last chapter tasks students with not only finding the one correct answer but also interacting in some manner with all of the distractors (wrong answers) provided. More interaction requires more cognition. This, in turn, leads to more learning and remembering. Ultimately, that is obviously the goal. No matter how you might structure retrieval practice, always focus on what and how the students are thinking with the material.

Unfortunately, I believe it is a general reaction and belief that more complex activities equal more cognition. That certainly isn't always true. Often times, as was mentioned in Part I, more complex activities may lead to students either confused and/or students focusing on the wrong aspects of the assignment. Some of the best assessments of knowledge are also the simplest in design and execution.

The Brain Dump

The brain dump certainly fits this description. It is simple in nature but allows students to do some great retrieval and even provides students with the cognitive freedom to access related information. This is something that I generally pose to students at the beginning of the class asking them to access information from past lessons in some way. It

DOI: 10.4324/9781003472056-13

is always an open-ended question, allowing students to write as much as they want to ensure they answer the question completely. Here's an example of a brain dump prompt:

> Explain the process of vision, including structures and their functions.

Students would read this and be tasked with "dumping their brain" of all information related. Students with the requisite knowledge and ability to construct a response describing the process of vision would definitely be demonstrating an understanding of the material. This is in contrast to possibly posing a question of the same topic this way:

> Describe the functions of the following structures of the eye:
>
> Iris - Cornea - Retina - Lens

This may seem like a somewhat negligible change, but the first option really provides a better opportunity for more working with the material to be retrieved from memory. With the bottom prompt, students have four very specific goals. Hopefully, students will know those four structures of the eye and their function(s). But, these instructions are somewhat limiting, especially if the goal of the assessment is to discuss as much about a somewhat expansive concept or procedure. Students will perform this task and nothing more. Don't get me wrong, if they can do this, that's fantastic…much better than not asking them to retrieve any information.

But, with the manner in which the first prompt is written, students may include the four structures and functions from the bottom prompt and then also include more information; perhaps they also state the functions of the pupil, rods, cones, bipolar cells, ganglion cells, et cetera. They still accomplished the goals of the bottom prompt, but also included so much more. They may also write their answer in a manner that describes vision as a process, explaining how these structures work together rather than as independent structures. This provides the ability to strengthen the schemas and associations surrounding the topic, which can make retrieval of all information more efficient later.

The Goal-Free Effect

Writing the brain dump prompt in this manner elicits what is called the *goal-free effect* of cognitive load theory.[1] With the second prompt, students have a very specific goal to meet, and when they do, they're done with the thinking and the assessment. With the first prompt, though, students are free of that specific goal and are free (and encouraged) to include any bits of information that contribute to answering the more open-ended question.

My biggest question with using the goal-free effect is this: *what if a student has no idea and cannot list any structures of the eye?* They're left doing nothing and not really strengthening their ability to retrieve any of the material while others are writing away. My potential solution to this problem: After a few minutes, supply a "cheat sheet" of sorts with terms they should have used. This will provide an opportunity for students to make sure they're on the right track and allow those who are out of ideas a prompt to get them working again. I plan on encouraging those who are going strong to avoid looking at the cheat sheet…if they don't need the crutch, they shouldn't use the crutch.

After I've given students enough time to complete the above, I want the students to have a quick conversation with their nearest peers… what terms/concepts did you include that other students did not? What terms/concepts did others include that you omitted? Then, finish up the review/assessment with some whole-class discussion of the topic to make sure we're all of the same understanding with respect to this topic.

Will the top prompt require more time than the bottom? Of course, but I believe the quality of work that students produce will be much better… they will be thinking more about the material. Instead of thinking of the different structures of the eye as independent bits of information, they will retrieve them as part of the process of vision and see how they all work together. Can or should the goal-free effect be applied to every opportunity for retrieval practice? Of course not. There are times where, as the teacher, I want to know (and I want the students to know) very specific answers and information. But, for more process or concept-oriented material, the goal-free effect is a strategy for allowing students to really think through and include as much related material as possible.

Color Coding Like Material

A last example of retrieval practice that really gets students comparing and contrasting information involves tasking students with color coding like material for concepts and/or events before using that same material to answer questions and/or construct a summary about the information. Here's an example from my class:

Social psychology experiments

1   Using the color code below, highlight the following terms if it refers to...

Zimbardo's experiment	Asch's experiment	Milgram's experiment

everyone agrees	role playing	Solomon Asch
shock generator	Yale University	obedience
Philip Zimbardo	60-65%	40 males
conformity	hunger strike	voltage
1963/1974	1955	37%

no role models for defiance	group of at least 3 people
victim is depersonalized	Stanford University
24 male college students	prisoners/prision guards
authority figure is close	feel incompetent
from a prestigious institution	aged 20-50

2   Confirm your highlighted terms with your notes, the textbook, and/or your peers.

3   Group your highlighted terms together and write a summary/review of all 3 experiments. Be sure to use all terms AND appropriately highlight the terms as they are used. This should be 3 different summaries/reviews.

Bonus - In a paragraph, describe ethical dilemmas that could/should be associated with some or all of the above experiments.

I typically use this for topics and concepts with a lot of facts, such as statistics, that students need to understand and be able to recall. The color-coding aspect (task one above) allows students to sort through and organize the many facts associated with the experiments; an important cognitive task. I ask students to first attempt this with no help (using Brain – Book – Buddy). Task two sees students use their notebook, textbook, and/or peers to ensure they have all of the facts appropriately sorted before moving to task three.

This task is really where students take their knowledge of the independent terms and statistics and apply them to construct a meaningful sequence of information. This is a more cognitively robust task than simply grouping the terms, but the initial organizing (task one) makes completion of the more difficult task more manageable on working memory and increases the students' likelihood of being successful.

What to Retrieve?

A last question I'm often asked about retrieval practice is "how do you decide what material to include on retrieval opportunities in class?" Such a valid question and speaks to one of, if not the most, precious resource in teaching...time. It is so limited and requires teachers consider how they will use it best. There just isn't enough time to do all of the things we wish we could with our students. So, retrieval of every single point made is simply impossible. Some material must be prioritized over other, and I have three criteria I use to help me sort through what to include:

Material That Is Critical for Seeing the Big Picture

Any information that is core to the major concepts in the class or particular unit we are studying are usually the first items I want to assess with my students. If they don't understand these crucial elements, it will be much more difficult for them to incorporate and understand other material. It is vital students encounter this material during reviews to provide several opportunities for retrieval.

Material That Relates to Today's Lesson

If there's information today that continues a thread of thought or really relates well to material covered at an earlier date, I love including it on these informal assessments. Not only does it capitalize on spaced practice of the older material and accessing relevant background knowledge, it is a great starting point for discussion in the class.

Having students chat about commonalities between two ideas, how this event led to the next, how one piece of writing is similar to another, or how a particular method in a math class builds on today's lesson can be a very worthwhile activity. You know as well as I that students tend to see content as compartmentalized and fractured; if it's a new chapter or unit, they see it as completely different. Sometimes that is true, but often there's some line of continuity that can be discovered and utilized in the classroom to link content.

Material That Is Commonly Confused

I know in my classroom there are many terms and concepts that may be confusing for students to remember correctly. For instance, with respect to interference and remembering, there's proactive interference and retroactive interference. Proactive interference occurs when old memories disrupt the retrieval of new memories. For example, when students move to a new grade in school, they may receive a new locker with a new combination.

At the start of the new year, students will probably struggle to recall their new combination from memory but be able to recall their old combination. Retroactive interference occurs when new memories disrupt the retrieval of old memories. After a few months of school, students will more likely be able to recall their new locker combination from memory but struggle to retrieve last year's locker combination. I know students struggle to correctly remember these terms, so I know I want to make sure we discuss them and students have multiple opportunities to retrieve this material.

Using these criteria really helps me to retrieve information that is most important for a complete understanding not only of the material to be covered today but also to clear up any misconceptions and to possibly access some background information on content for the future.

I've spent a great number of words and pages lauding the importance of retrieval practice...and I don't regret it. Without a doubt, when done correctly, retrieval practice is one of the most powerful tools in the teacher's bag of tricks. I cannot imagine an effective or efficient classroom or study setting without utilizing retrieval practice. Assessment, in some form, is necessary in a successful classroom. And, generally speaking, the more opportunities we provide for students to retrieve information, the better.

Note

1 Sweller, J., Ayres, P., & Kalyuga, S. (2011). The goal-free effect. In J. M. Spector & Susanne P. Lajoie (Eds.), *Cognitive load theory. Explorations in the learning sciences, instructional systems and performance technologies* (Vol. 1, pp. 89–98). Springer.

11 Introduction to Spaced Practice

There is another learning strategy that is right up there with respect to its ability to positively influence learning in the classroom. It is usually either called spaced practice or distributed practice. While retrieval practice looks at *what* and *how* the students think about the material, spaced practice considers *when* this retrieval occurs. And, just like there are several different methods to implement retrieval practice, spaced practice can be utilized in numerous ways. There's also over 100 years of research into this learning strategy, so it has been widely studied.[1]

So, what is spaced practice? Well, it is the opposite of the ever popular "cramming" for a test. With cramming, students usually spend a substantial amount of time the night before an assessment attempting to "cram" the information into their brain. For many different reasons, this usually leads to poor results and a frustrated learner.

Spaced practice takes those same hours of studying the night before the test and spreads them out over a number of days. Students may spend the same amount of time preparing for a test, but by spacing out the studying, not only will students probably be less frustrated, they will probably also see better results on the assessment.[2]

DOI: 10.4324/9781003472056-14

Cramming

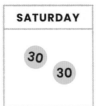

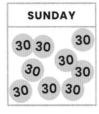

Spacing

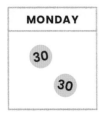

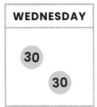

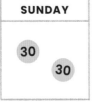

This effect has been demonstrated hundreds of times in both the lab and classroom setting. One such experiment had students learning mathematical permutations via either spaced practice or massed practice (cramming).[3] All participants viewed a tutorial that included explanatory information and a sample problem, with a verbal explanation of the content. During week one of the experiment and after the tutorial, all participants completed a first set of practice problems, composed of two examples and two practice problems.

The participants in the massed practice group then immediately worked a second set of two problems. The spaced practice participants did not work on the second set yet. A week later (week two), after attempting both sets of practice problems, the massed practice participants took an assessment and their performance was recorded. During this same session a week later, the spaced practice participants now attempted the second set of practice problems. Then, a week after that (week three), the spaced practice group took the assessment and their scores were recorded.

The results? *The spaced practice participants averaged 74%, while the massed practice averaged 49% on the final assessment.*

A   Practice procedure

	Spacers	Massers	Light Massers
Week 1	2 problems	4 problems	2 problems
Week 2	2 problems	Test	Test
Week 3	Test	Filler task	Filler task

B   Test performance

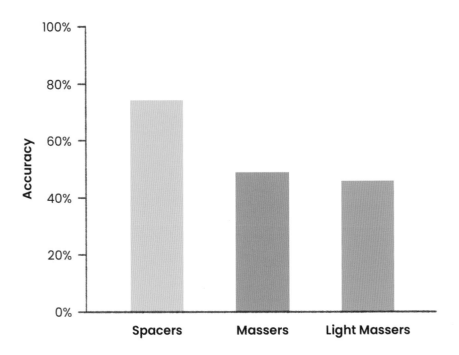

That is quite a difference in scores. Did the spaced practice group study longer or prepare with more practice problems than the massed practice group? No. Before learning about the power of spaced practice, I think my intuition would lead me to believe the spaced practice group would perform worse due to the week of space between their two sessions of practice before waiting another week before the assessment...but that is simply not so. There is something very powerful, from a cognitive perspective, with allowing time for forgetting before restudying a particular concept.

In another study, researchers found that students who intuitively employed spaced practice earned higher grades on end of unit tests than those who crammed or massed practice as their method of study.[4]

An overwhelming majority of students do not naturally use spaced practice, so finding those who do is a bit of an anomaly. Also, interestingly enough, the students in this study who benefited most from using spaced practice were lower ability students and less likely to use spaced practice. This research highlights a couple of important points about the use of spaced practice.

Student's Intuition about How to Study Does Not Lend Itself to Using Spaced Practice

As was mentioned earlier when discussing the student use of retrieval practice, teachers cannot expect students to just use spaced practice because it is more beneficial. We need to lead conversations with students about these effects and model with them, in class, how to employ spaced practice. With my students, I will even show them research on these effects so they see this isn't necessarily just one more thing their teacher wants them to do. There are real and very tangible benefits not only in this class but in all of their classes now and in the future.

Spaced Practice Benefits All Learners, Especially Lower Ability Students

As with retrieval practice, spacing out studying does not simply improve those who are already probably going to do well in the classroom. Both spaced and retrieval practice benefits all learners, especially those who may struggle the most.

These two points are so important for students and teachers to understand. In the classroom, unfortunately, I think sometimes teachers are given a deluge of tasks to complete from people outside their classroom. We are often not told why we need to do these things, but just that we need to get them done or complete them with our students. I know I've developed a sort of apathy for these tasks and just complete them to get them over with. I can only imagine students feel the same way when living up to different teachers' expectations and following their procedures.

Explicitly showing students *why* studying using spaced practice (and retrieval practice) is so much more beneficial than more passive methods or cramming, I believe, elicits more by-in from students. I remember when I began doing this, the students' appreciation for sort of including them in the process of "why" was a bit eye opening for them and me. Many didn't really realize they were going through the motions of studying and learning. Treating my students in a more scholarly manner positively impacted their outlook on their learning and, I believe, helped to create better studying and learning habits.

How Much Spacing?

But how much spacing is enough spacing? How much time should students leave between restudy attempts and a final assessment? Well, there is also research on this. [5] And, while there are statistics that provide an approximate ideal time between studying and assessment ("20 percent of the test delay for delays of a few weeks"), I don't think, as a teacher, that getting to that level of application of spaced practice is reasonable for the classroom. Even the authors of the article state this:

> The optimally efficient gap between study sessions is not some absolute quantity that can be recommended, but a quantity that depends dramatically upon the retention interval. To put it simply, if you want to know the optimal distribution of study time, you need to decide how long you wish to remember something.

This study looked all the way out at retention for years and found delaying the spacing of several months to produce a positive retention rate of information. In most classrooms, though, while wanting students to remember information for...forever is an aspiration, in reality, we cannot space practice of content for months. Our curriculums and pacing guides dictate we must continue moving forward for a school year, rendering spaced practice of two to three months of material to be quite impractical.

However, for assessments that may be a week or two away, delaying practice for 20% of that timeframe is quite realistic. But again, I say (as a person who loves to nerd out about statistics), I don't find it advantageous to have this "I should wait until 20% of the time has elapsed before providing an opportunity in class for my students to study" to be helpful. Any spacing is better than no spacing. Just like any retrieval is better than no retrieval. Or, as I'll say to my students occasionally, "a little bit of something is better than a lot of nothing."

Notes

1 Ebbinghaus, H. (1913). Memory (H. A. Ruger & C. E. Bussenius, Trans.). Teachers College, Columbia University. (Original work published 1885)

2 Adapted from Hendrick and Caviglioli's *"Wellington School Study Guide."*

3 Rohrer, D., & Taylor, K. (2007). The shuffling of mathematics problems improves learning. *Instructional Science, 35*, 481-498.

4 Carvalho, P. F., Sana, F., & Yan, V. X. (2020). Self-regulated spacing in a massive open online course is related to better learning. *NPJ Science of Learning, 5*(1), 2.

5 Cepeda, N. J., Vul, E., Rohrer, D., Wixted, J. T., & Pashler, H. (2008). Spacing effects in learning: A temporal ridgeline of optimal retention. *Psychological Science, 19*(11), 1095-1102.

12 The Exit Ticket and Last Lesson, Last Week, Last Month

So, as a teacher who knows about the long-term benefits of spaced retrieval, how does this shape my practice? How do I apply this to my classroom instruction? Well, almost immediately, I employ this knowledge to how I administer exit tickets in my classroom. The exit ticket is used often as a quick method for assessing student understanding and performance for a (usually) simple task. For those of you who may be unfamiliar with the exit ticket, they usually work something like this:

Improving upon the Exit Ticket

As students pack up their things and prepare to leave the classroom, they are provided a sticky note, an index card, or maybe just a quarter sheet of paper. The teacher poses a question from the current lesson that usually requires a short response. Students are to jot down their answer and leave it somewhere (stuck to the board or maybe in a basket) on their way out. Their answer is their ticket to exit.

Teachers look at these tickets to gauge student understanding of the material presented. If, in general, the class performs well, maybe tomorrow's lesson will include less class time reviewing this material. If, in general, the class performs poorly, the teacher may begin class with a more substantial rehashing of the material before moving on. And, of course, students who leave the class answering the question, they believe, correctly develop a sense of "I understand this information and I've got it."

DOI: 10.4324/9781003472056-15

Simple, yet effective...or so it seems. But maybe there is a problem with this traditional usage of the exit ticket. When assessment occurs during or immediately following a lesson, we receive a somewhat inaccurate measure of what students know. These almost immediate assessments would more accurately portray student performance, and not so much learning.

From research by Bjork and Bjork,[1] it is important to understand the difference between performance and learning. Performance is "what we can observe and measure during instruction or training." Learning is "the more or less permanent change in knowledge or understanding that is the target of instruction." In other words, performance is what we can do in the moment, and learning is what we can recall after a more extended period of time.

Learning vs Performance

Learning is ...	Performance is ...
Long-term change in knowledge and understanding.	Short-term, temporary and observable reflection on current ability.
No judgement.	Feel judged or assessed.
Measured against previous self.	Measured against others.
Low pressure.	High pressure.
Emphasis on improving yourself.	Emphasis on proving yourself.
Done in private or public.	Often done in public.
Development is the primary reward.	Winning is the primary reward.

When assessment occurs during or immediately following a lesson, we're not really finding out what students know. In reality, this only shows whether a student was paying attention and could regurgitate the material somewhat immediately. Now, don't get me wrong, selectively attending to the presentation of material is a necessity for learning, but it isn't everything. It is a step in the process of learning.

If teachers use exit tickets traditionally, they may inaccurately assume students properly understand information they really don't. Students have performed well, but true learning hasn't necessarily occurred. This assumption of learning can have a negative effect on the classroom both in the moment and during the planning of future lessons.

Obviously, in the classroom, performance is not the goal. True, honest assessment and learning are what we strive to provide.

So, how can the exit ticket be improved upon? How can it be a more effective assessment of learning?

1) **Allow time for forgetting.** The main problem with the traditional usage of the exit ticket is that there's no time to forget, which leads to the measuring of performance and not learning. Contrary to popular belief, allowing for time to forget actually creates a more beneficial scenario for a more accurate assessment of learning. So, instead of using an exit ticket to assess that day's lesson, why not ask what they remember from a previous lesson?

   I find this is incredibly effective if that information ties in to what was covered in class that day. So, maybe in a history classroom, instead of asking for facts about a battle of the Civil War that was covered that day in class, you ask students to remember what actions lead to the start of the battle, which was taught a few lessons before.

2) **Opt for an entrance ticket.** Instead of assessing the day's lesson as they leave, provide students with an index card (or sticky note or whatever) on their way in the next day and assess their knowledge then. Asking those same questions 24 hours after the lesson is much more indicative of their true level of understanding and makes better use of spacing out their practice. It also provides a wonderful opportunity at the beginning of a lesson to link yesterday's material to the present day's content.

3) **Ask for predictions.** As they exit, instead of asking about what they learned that day, ask for predictions of where they think tomorrow's lesson is going. What's next? And, while this sort of predicting lends itself more to some disciplines than others, it can be a really effective method for starting a class discussion the next day..."Ally, you

wrote on your exit ticket yesterday, that you believe the soldiers will next retreat and search for provisions. What makes you think that?"

While we don't really need to throw the baby out with the bathwater as it pertains to exit tickets, there are more efficient and effective ways to use them. Along with improving upon the exit ticket and perhaps turning it more into an entrance ticket, there needs to be a discussion with students about why this is better for retention of material. That's where talk of spacing out studying is more advantageous for learning. It may not feel as good to allow for some forgetting, but the accuracy of an informal or formative assessment is much higher when retrieval is distributed, rather than crammed.

Last Lesson, Last Week, Last Month

A really useful activity I use in my classroom that makes explicit usage of spaced retrieval practice is called Last Lesson, Last Week, Last Month. The name pretty much tells you what's going on. I select anywhere from two to five questions about information that was taught during the last lesson, about a week ago, and about a month ago. You don't have to be super strict on exactly how long ago the information was taught with respect to last week and last month. I've seen other teachers take this and accommodate it for their classes and question information from one unit and two units in the past. It all works. It's all spacing of information.

Last lesson, last week, last month

1st attempt = Brain	2nd attempt = Notebook	3rd attempt = Buddy

Last lesson

1   Define consciousness

2   List the 4 stages of sleep in order and provide one characteristic of each stage.

3   Describe as many theories for why we sleep as you can.

Last week

1   What does it mean to encode information?

2   What types of information do we automatically encode?

3   Chunking, mnemonics, and hierarchies are all processing strategies. Describe what they are and discuss how they help with learning.

Last month

1   Why should we not always trust our intuition?

2   Which correlation coefficient represents the strongest relationship:

   A. -.71   B. .38   C. 1.06   D. -.93

3   Explain what a placebo is and how/why it is used in experimentation.

There are a few aspects of this activity that are quite powerful for learning outside of the obvious positive impact of spaced retrieval practice:

1) It reminds students of how important it is to revisit older content, as it is still relevant to their understanding of current and future material. Often times, students will forget some of the content from a week and month ago, but with a little feedback, they usually reply with a sort of "oh yeah, I remember us talking about that" response.

   This does a good job to remind students that just because they may have known and understood the material a month ago for a particular assessment, that doesn't mean it is remembered forever. Again, forgetting occurs with all learners. However, spaced retrieval of that material creates a greater possibility that it will be stored for a longer period of time and more easily accessed when needed.

2) If there is a common thread to unify these questions in different units of study, it provides for a powerful discussion of how the topics all compare and contrast. For instance, in a history class where information is traditionally studied chronologically, seeing how decisions made in the content a month ago led to the topics a week ago and now to what was learned in the lesson yesterday...really good stuff and not something students intuitively consider or realize. The same could be said for processes in math class, where concepts learned a month ago may need to be mastered before completing more recent content. It could really help to identify deficiencies in students' understanding of how to solve problems.

   In an English class, how are the protagonists in these three readings similar and how are they different? With a little accommodating for each teacher's particular content and class, last lesson, last week, and last month can be quite powerful for remembering and for creating new context and application of that learning.

A few years ago, using the Last Lesson, Last Week, Last Month activity created one of the more powerful moments of insight with respect to actually seeing the benefits of spaced retrieval practice. A real "ah-ha" moment for myself and my students. We don't get too many of those, so it's really nice to see the impact of what you're doing in class playing out for your students.

Let me ask you a question, remembering that the questions that are now in the last month category were once in the last week category and the last lesson category. The questions in the last week category were once in the last lesson category. The questions in the last lesson category were only presented during instruction around 24 hours ago before they were posed to the students. If you look back at the image of Last Lesson, Last Week, Last Month from a few pages ago, which set of three questions do you believe a class of 30 students would perform best on and which set do you believe they would perform worst on? I wondered this one day in class and decided to "run the numbers" and see.

My intuition led me to believe my students would score better on the last lesson questions and score the worst on the last month questions, since that lesson was taught the longest ago and there had been so much time for forgetting of information. However, that was not the case at all. In actuality, students performed the best on the last month questions and the worst on the last week questions.

This was totally unexpected. In my mind, the last lesson should have been the strongest of knowledge because that content is only 24 hours old, and the last month should've been the weakest and the most forgotten because it was the oldest.

What in the world happened? I was a bit dumbfounded until I really considered, from a cognitive perspective, what was going on.

The three questions in the last month category were first experienced in class, then retrieved the next day (last lesson questions), then retrieved again the next week (last week questions), and finally retrieved one more time (last month questions). That doesn't take into account what other studying and retrieving of that information students might have done during their own studying for quizzes and tests along the way. That's a lot of retrieving making that material much stronger in the students' memory. So, it really makes sense that it would be the strongest and most easily retrieved.

The three questions in the last week category were obviously experienced in class and then again as last lesson questions. But then they were probably not considered or minimally thought of for the next five or six days, leaving ample time for a lot of forgetting. From that point of view, it makes sense that those questions were remembered the worst. Probably not enough effortful retrieval of that information to really solidify the content long term.

The three questions in the last lesson category are, more or less, fresh in the memories of the students (although, a lot of forgetting may occur in 24 hours). So, again, it seems logical those questions would be remembered relatively well versus those questions asking about information from content presented and/or retrieved more distantly.

The results of this barely scientific bit of research in my classroom spoke to me for a couple of reasons:

1) Just like I would tell my students, you cannot always trust your intuition when it comes to the academic setting. We all come to the table (or desk) with our own conscious and unconscious biases about the world around us. This includes our assumptions about learning and education. These results were a surprise to me because I had already formed my opinion of what the results would be. Now, there's nothing really wrong with that as long as I am aware I shouldn't make decisions in the classroom based upon those assumptions and should look for evidence to either confirm or refute my beliefs.

2) This provided for an absolutely wonderful discussion with my students. They experienced the results of this research in real time, just like their teacher. And, they appeared to be just as flummoxed as I. Don't discount the benefit of students seeing teachers learning along the way. I believe I've gotten more buy-in from students in class because they see me reading research and attempting pseudo-research to test results. They know I care about doing what is best for their learning and enjoy participating in both discussions about human learning and experimenting with what works and what potentially doesn't work.

Note

1 Bjork, E. L., & Bjork, R. A. (2011). Making things hard on yourself, but in a good way: Creating desirable difficulties to enhance learning. In M. A. Gernsbacher, R. W. Pew, L. M. Hough, & J. R. Pomerantz (Eds.), *Psychology and the real world: Essays illustrating fundamental contributions to society* (pp. 59–68). Worth Publishers.

13 Student Intuition, Modeling, and Framing Forgetting

With little doubt, over a century of research into learning indicates the two learning strategies that seem to provide the most positive effects for a large majority of students are the two mentioned in this book: retrieval practice and spaced practice. I put more time into introducing these strategies and cultivating students' ability to efficiently and effectively use them both within class and outside class; whether that be at home studying or in other classes.

As has already been mentioned, the great thing about these strategies is that they absolutely are not specific to one age range or ability level or type of content. They are for the benefit of all learners and should be embedded early in the school setting because these strategies are not intuitive. Humans don't look to use retrieval practice for learning. Unfortunately, in our system of education, any type of assessment is usually only viewed by students as an end to learning and not as a part of that process. It is a snapshot of what someone knows at that moment, but by attempting to retrieve the material in that moment and potentially receiving feedback on the work, learning has occurred and a subsequent assessment of the same content would tend to yield more positive results than the first assessment.

Student Intuition

But again, I say, that's not how students have been taught to perceive assessments. That certainly needs to change. In a 2009 study[1], researchers asked 177 college students the following question:

DOI: 10.4324/9781003472056-16

What kind of strategies do you use when you are studying? List as many strategies as you use and rank-order them from strategies you use most often to strategies you use least often.

The results? Repeated rereading was by far the most frequently listed strategy (84% reported using) and 55% reported that it was their number one strategy used. Only 11% reported practicing recall (self-testing) of information and 1% identified practicing recall as their number one strategy. This indicates to me a majority of students do not make great choices when it comes to studying with only one out of one hundred using the most efficient and effective learning strategy.

I am going to liberally apply these results to younger students, too. It seems highly unlikely to me that students would learn healthy study habits while in their earlier days of schooling and suddenly stop using them when college begins. I believe most are never taught proper study habits and choose the path of least resistance. While rereading and highlighting may exhaust time while studying, it often utilizes little cognition. And, it is just not fun to apply spaced retrieval practice and find out you don't know something, as often happens when using these strategies. It is much more pleasing and easier to reread notes and highlight a few key words along the way. But, as I frequently tell my students:

> You'd rather find out before the test that you don't know something. If you find out on the final assessment that you don't know or understand a concept or a term, it's too late. Get the "oh wow, I didn't know I needed to know that" out of the way during studies using spaced retrieval practice so there are no surprises on assessment day.

When to Introduce Learning Strategies to Students?

So, knowing that my students do not intuitively study (and have probably never been taught) in the most efficient or effective manner, how and when do I introduce spaced practice and retrieval practice in my classroom? The answers? Day one with learning their names. Needing (and wanting) to learn my student's names as quickly as possible is a task that requires explicit effort, exactly like the information students learn most days in school. So, I think it incredibly advantageous, as I begin talking to them about retrieval practice and spaced practice, that I model what this actual looks like.

This process takes, on average, five minutes per class; utilizing more time in the earlier days and quickly tailing off to just a couple of minutes by day five and six. Here's the process with commentary on what I say to my students throughout the week or so of learning their names:

Day 1 - *Initial attendance call and asking students the name they prefer to be called. Students create a name tag.*

I think it's important that students are called by a name that they like. I'm sure you don't know (and why would you?), but my first name is Augustus. I tell my students that I obviously didn't go by Augustus in school or I'd still be stuffed in a locker somewhere. So, while in school, I was always called Blake, my middle name. I understand those that wish to be something other than their first name. Also, I emphasize with students to not let me call them the wrong name...correct me (politely) whenever I accidentally mispronounce or completely use the incorrect name.

At this point, I also have students make a name tag out of an index card and have them fold it in half and place it on their desk in front of them. The name they wish to be called should be large, and their last name should be smaller. For most of the process, I have students place this card in front of them during class as a "cheat sheet" for me at the beginning. I take them up at the end of class and have them pick them up at the beginning of class the next day. Eventually, as you'll see, I have them turn these down so I cannot use them as a crutch. This is a great example of diminishing cues retrieval practice.

At this point, my discussion of learning strategies centers around why I need to practice to learn my 90 students' names. This is not implicit knowledge. This learning is effortful, like much of the school work they will experience in my class and all of their other classes. So, I am setting up a system to effectively study a little every day to eventually know all of the names. I cannot rely on simply rereading the class roster over and over again and expect quality results (like students rereading their notes before an assessment). I need to really put forth effort and risk getting student's names wrong in order to eventually get them correct. It's okay if I don't know their names for the first week or so of class...that is to be expected. But if we get to a month in and I still don't know their name, that's a problem and it's my fault. Much of studying is the same way.

I expect students to not know everything by memory after they first encounter it in class, and they'd rather get it incorrect on low or no stakes formative assessment during class or during their personal studying opportunities than finding out on the summative assessment they don't know some information. At that time, it may be too late to correct any misconceptions or fill any gaps in their knowledge.

Day 2 – *Students place their name tag in front of them face down to start class. I use the printed class roster to try and match students with their names...and fail miserably for the most part. After this, I have students put their name tags up for the remainder of class so I can reference them.*

There is a lot of failure in success, and this is where students begin to see the real work of studying and the failure that may accompany it. In a class of 30, I may remember five or so at this point...and that's ok. Again, it is to be expected that I don't know all of their names after first meeting them yesterday. I point out that I do have the class roster to use as a way of making this retrieval a matching attempt. I am not just blindly coming up with names, but I know that someone in this class is named "Michael"...but who is it?

And, I reiterate some of what I talked about with them on day 1; why I'm attempting to retrieve names, why I'd rather fail now to succeed later, why this is very similar to how they should study, et cetera. Also, on day 2, I introduce the idea of spaced practice. Rather than just cramming the practice of learning their names into one day, I should space out that practice across many days for a few minutes. That will lead to better results. Allow time for forgetting. If not, I might create a false sense of how many names I know. And, of course, when cramming for assessments, students do the same thing. They study for an hour or two the night before a test and believe they know it and are surprised the next day when they cannot recall the answers on the test and say something like, "but I studied for two hours last night!" Cramming may lead to better immediate results, but spacing study attempts is much more efficient and effective for long-term retention of material.

Day 3 - *Repeat the steps in day 2.*

There's not a lot of change in the implementation between day 2 and day 3. Students should (hopefully) see me remember more names correctly in day 3's attempt to match names from the roster with the student. This stimulates some discussion of how multiple retrieval attempts across time (spaced practice) will demonstrate improved results; still not perfect, but improvement is a step in the right direction.

Day 4 - *Instead of students getting their name tag, I attempt to pass them out from a random order. Then, depending on how I feel, I may ask them to either keep their name tag up or keep it turned down for the remainder of class.*

Once again, students should see me struggling a little less and seeing more success in retrieving names. Passing out the name tags in a random order may seem like a small change, but I become accustomed to seeing their names in order and that biases who I try to match the name tag with. By seeing them in a random order (another context), it increases the difficulty, but also strengthens the connections between name and student.

This begins the discussion of studying material in different contexts. It's one thing to know the definition of a term because you've read the term and definition five times...it's another thing to see that term used in a paragraph and have the ability to know what it means within that different context. Eventually, this leads to a talk about near and far transfer of learning, which is incredibly important for understanding and application.

Day 5 - *Have students get their name tag and immediately turn them down so I cannot see them. I attempt to recall their names without any help, using only my brain.*

This represents a shift in how I am attempting to retrieve the information of student's names. Up to this point, I have been drawing from a list of names or the name tag...basically recognition of information (like matching or multiple-choice questions). Today, there is no help. Instead of recognition, now I am using recall. This is, cognitively, a much more difficult task. I may forget some of the names that I knew yesterday, but that is okay. Again, forgetting happens. I will be better off in the long run by gradually increasing the difficulty of this activity.

This also opens up talk of which is truer assessment of one's knowledge, recognition questions or recall questions. I may be able to "cheat" by guessing on recognition attempts, but it is much more difficult to do so with recall questions. I can either answer the question or I cannot. I can either recall the student's name or I cannot. And, while this may be an uncomfortable realization, I'd rather find out now that I do not know their names so I can continue to practice during class.

Day 6 - *No name tags. No roster. I ask students to sit in a different seat and beside different students at the beginning of class when I try to identify all the students by name.*

Okay. This is the real deal. All crutches I might have been using are now gone. And, I've made it more difficult by having students sit in different seats, surrounded by different students. This continues the conversation of attempting to retrieve information in different contexts. If I can retrieve their names today, I can feel pretty confident that I really have that information. (How many times have you known the name of a student when they are sitting in your classroom but draw a blank when you see them in the hallway? Different contexts.) Similarly, if students can retrieve and apply content in different contexts, that is a good indicator they really know their stuff.

Usually, by this point, I am at 100% and students ceremoniously throw their name tag in the trash...although some strangely choose to keep theirs. Thus concludes my modeling of spaced retrieval practice to learn my students' names. I usually have one final discussion with them where we think back on the different steps from day 1 to day 6. They see me struggling at the beginning but getting better with more attempts. They see me having mental crutches at the beginning (class roster printed and name tags up) and slowly see those crutches removed. They see that my "studying" of names doesn't have to take long; only taking around five minutes every class meeting.

There are so many positives that come out of this that, I believe, help to create a nice classroom environment for learning and demonstrate to students how learning is a process that may require some help and forgetting along the way.

Framing Forgetting

And about forgetting...how we talk about this and how our students think about it in the classroom and within the framework of learning needs a bit of a change. I feel confident in saying that the concept generally has a negative connotation in our society. And I get it. When I forget my coffee at home or can't remember where I placed my phone, I'm certainly not jumping for joy at the forgetting. And don't get me started on forgetting passwords to different websites and apps that all have different requirements for those passwords. You literally have to admit to your forgetting by clicking a *Forgot Password* link. Forgetting can certainly be a disruption and negatively impact our mood and ability to complete tasks.

But, within the confines of memory and learning, I don't believe that negative undertone is warranted. Forgetting is the norm in our life. For many different reasons, we forget. Our brains, as amazing as they are, are fallible. And it doesn't really matter how much we try to focus and selectively attend to information, some of it will be forgotten. The research on forgetting is pretty straightforward:

The course of forgetting is initially rapid, then levels off with time.

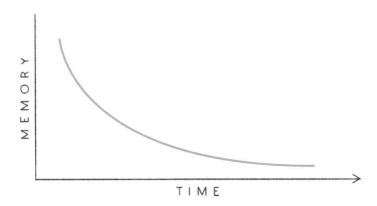

We forget a lot of information quickly after initially coming into contact with it so forgetting isn't the exception to the rule...it is the rule.

But is that how forgetting is framed in education, though? Do we normally see it as something that is a normal part of life? From my perspective and experience, I don't think so. Forgetting is bad. Forgetting could possibly lead to a reduction in grade or could indicate "you didn't try hard enough" in class. This can lead to feelings of frustration and judgement. And, for the most part, because it is seen as bad, we don't really talk about it other than to say, "study more" with no further guidance.

We need to work to change this narrative with our students and present forgetting as something to be expected, but not necessarily lauded. Let the students in on this secret of forgetting and memory. Tell them forgetting is normal and expected. And the reason we're doing these formative assessments (spaced retrieval practice) is to simply indicate what you do remember and what you've forgotten so future studying can be more efficient and effective. And please mention this often: "Remember, I don't expect you to know everything and you shouldn't either. You should have forgotten some of this. We just want to highlight what you know and what you don't know so you and I can better tailor class instruction and studying."

This is probably a paradigm shift for students. So, just telling them once won't help to reshape their beliefs and habits...it needs to be mentioned often. When students don't see formative assessment as a threat but as simply an assessment of what they remember, they are more likely to participate, provide an honest attempt, and reap the benefits of spaced retrieval practice.

Note

1   Karpicke, J. D., Butler, A. C., & Roediger III, H. L. (2009). Metacognitive strategies in student learning: Do students practise retrieval when they study on their own? *Memory, 17*(4), 471–479.

Part II Major Points

- Over a century of research points to two widely applicable strategies to maximize learning.

- Honest assessment of students' knowledge is essential in an effective classroom.

- Retrieval practice is a way to identify what students know and don't know while also strengthening the memories of the information recalled.

- Retrieval practice can reduce test anxiety and produce stress resistant memories.

- Spaced practice has been shown much more effective for long-term retention of material over cramming.

- There is evidence spaced retrieval practice greatly improves learning for lower ability students.

- Student's intuition for how to properly study is often flawed.

- Explicit conversations with students and modeling of the use and benefits of spaced practice and retrieval practice are needed.

- Forgetting is normal. It is part of the learning process.

DOI: 10.4324/9781003472056-17

Conclusion

As a teacher, learning about the information covered in this book revolutionized how I thought about learning and conducted instruction in my classroom. As the quote stated in the introduction to Part I, my instructional design was blind due to my ignorance of memory processing and research surrounding more advantageous learning strategies like retrieval practice and spaced practice.

I spent the first decade of my teaching career doing what I thought was best, but was woefully oblivious to the application of cognitive psychology in the classroom. It took a somewhat serendipitous meeting on Twitter and taking a risk to begin my journey to being a better, more informed teacher. Today, my classroom environment and instruction are more organized, efficient, and effective. Maybe more importantly, I am able to have more intelligent and informed conversations with my students to make them more successful learners, not only in my class, but for the rest of their life.

My sincere hope is that this book does the same for you. I hope you now have a better understanding of how we learn and of certain choke points and pitfalls that may befall instruction and learning along the way. I hope you have several ideas for how to implement retrieval practice and spaced practice effectively in your classroom. I hope you feel a little relieved by the fact that simple and organized classrooms and instruction are superior to attempting to do all the things and apply all the bells and whistles. And I hope your students will be more motivated about learning and better understand how all of this impacts them directly now and in the future.

DOI: 10.4324/9781003472056-18

Index

Note: Page numbers in *italics* refer to figures.

Did you love reading about the research on Attention and Memory?

Want to get **amazing online training for your staff** that can take their understanding even further?

Then

The **Teacher CPD Academy**

is for you!

Simply scan this QR code

Or head over to
teacherCPDacademy.com

Or email
info@innerdrive.co.uk

to request a free trial.

We **illuminate research** with **inspiring** and **interactive** modules, interviews and keynote talks.

So, do not hesitate. A **brilliant professional development platform** for all your colleagues is only a click away!